# THE PERILS OF
# PERFECTION

**MAGENTA**
Bold Christian voices healing divides

## Living the Feminist Dream
A Faithful Vision for Women
in the Church and the World
Kate Bryan

## Keep at it, Riley!
Accompanying my Father
through Death into Life
Noreen Madden McInnes

## Rehumanize
A Vision to Secure Human Rights for All
Aimee Murphy

## The Church's Mission in a Polarized World
Aaron Wessman

## The Perils of Perfection
On the Limits and Possibilities of Human Enhancement
Joseph Vukov

# THE PERILS OF PERFECTION

## On the Limits and Possibilities of Human Enhancement

Joseph Vukov

NCP
NEW CITY PRESS

Published by New City Press
202 Comforter Blvd.,
Hyde Park, NY 12538
www.newcitypress.com

The Perils of Perfection
On the Limits and Possibilities of Human Enhancement

Cover by Maria Oswalt
Layout by Miguel Tejerina

ISBN: 978-1-56548-560-0 (Paperback)
ISBN: 978-1-56548-561-7 (E-book)

Library of Congress Control Number: 2023934065

For my children.

# Contents

Series Preface........................................................................... 9

Introduction........................................................................... 13

Chapter 1
**New Technologies of Human Enhancement**..................... 21

Chapter 2
**Humanity+**........................................................................ 47

Chapter 3
**Luddism Modernized**......................................................... 79

Chapter 4
**Fallen Dignity**................................................................. 116

Chapter 5
**Enhancing Humanity**........................................................ 150

Conclusion
**Enhancement and the Good Life**........................................ 170

Acknowledgements.............................................................. 177

Notes................................................................................. 179

m

# Series Preface

**D**oes the book that you are about to read seem unusual? Perhaps even counterintuitive?

Good. The Magenta series wouldn't be doing its job if you felt otherwise.

On the color wheel, magenta lies directly between red and blue. Just so, books in this series do not lie at one limit or another of our hopelessly simplistic, two-dimensional, antagonistic, binary imagination. Often, in the broader culture any answer to a moral or political question gets labeled as liberal or conservative, red or blue. But the Magenta series refuses to play by these shortsighted rules. Magenta will address the complexity of the issues of our day by resisting a framework that unnecessarily pits one idea against another. Magenta refuses to be defined by anything other than a positive vision of the good.

If you understand anything about the Focolare's dialogical-and-faithful mission, it should not surprise you that this series has found a home with the Focolare's New City Press. The ideas in these books, we believe, will spark dialogues that will heal divides and build unity at the very sites of greatest fragmentation and division.

The ideas in Magenta are crucial not only for our fragmented culture, but also for the Church. Our secular idolatry— our simplistic left/right, red/blue imagination— has oozed into the Church as well, disfiguring the Body of Christ with ugly disunity. Such idolatry, it must be said, has muffled the Gospel and crippled the Church, keeping it from being salt and light in a wounded world desperate for unity.

Magenta is not naïve. We realize full well that appealing to dialogue or common ground can be dismissed as a weak-sauce, milquetoast attempt to cloud our vision of the good or reduce it to a mere least common denominator. We know that much dialogic spade work is yet to be done, but that does not keep the vision of the Magenta Series (like the color it bears) from being *bold*. There is nothing half-hearted about it. All our authors have a brilliant, attractive vision of the good.

It is difficult to imagine a more timely and therefore important book than this one delivered by Joe Vukov. As the issues surrounding technology and human enhancement continue to explode onto the scene in nearly every aspect of our lives—from sexual performance to standardized test-taking—the debates over these technologies are predictably coalescing into two polarized camps. One camp is basically "technological progress no matter what!" while the other camp is skeptical of any transformation of the human being at all. And, as usual, they define themselves by opposition to each other.

Into this mess wades Professor Vukov—someone who manages to be a careful philosopher, engaging writer, and a faithful, non-ideological Christian. He has produced a powerful argument (one which, like all Magenta books, relies a series of powerful stories) based on both reason and theological commitment for a via media which puts significant limits on these technologies while at the same time making space for a Christian vision of human enhancement. Dear reader, you are in for a treat!

Enjoy!

Charles C. Camosy
Series Editor

# Introduction

Welcome to the future. Start with a stop at Tesla, Inc. No, not to buy a new car, but rather for a conversation the company's eccentric CEO, Elon Musk. Musk, one of the wealthiest people in the world, also mans the helm of Twitter, SpaceX, and The Boring Company. But that's not why we are here. Instead, we're here to discuss one of Musk's newest ventures: Neuralink.

Neuralink, launched in August 2020 with all the hoopla we've come to expect, has been touted as a "Fitbit for the brain." Its feature product: a type of brain-computer interface (BCI), a device implanted into the brain and linked to a computer. The immediate applications of Neuralink: to "help people with paralysis regain independence through control of computers and mobile devices."[1] A laudable goal, and one that would mark a milestone in assistive devices. Indeed, even before Musk applied Silicon Valley veneer to BCIs, scientists had developed technology that allows wheelchair-users to operate their chairs directly with their brains and people with quadriplegia to manipulate computer interfaces. Musk, however, lets us know that the plan isn't to stop here. Eventually, Musk hopes, Neuralink will allow users to "give people the ability to communicate more easily via text or speech synthesis, to follow their curiosity on the web, or to express their creativity through photography, art, or writing apps."[2] Move a cursor on your computer by thinking about it; control your iPhone with a thought; order an Uber by reflecting on your destination.

The end game of Neuralink? Musk is mum. But you needn't spend your spare time penning sci-fi novels to conjure possibilities. Imagine piloting a car simply by visualizing your destination. Or downloading the latest dance craze to shine at the wedding reception. Or mastering calculus with the click of a button. And the more sinister side of things? Again, you needn't have a well-developed dystopian vision to picture possibilities. All your data, sold to hungry marketers and transformed to ads beamed directly to your stream of consciousness. Government agencies, preventing "thought crime" by requisitioning Musk's servers. A vast social chasm opening between "linkers" and "non-linkers." Neuralink, you conclude, presents nothing short of revolutionary possibilities.

Let's move on. Our next stop is a rapid-fire tour of startups run by so-called "immortalists" or "healthspanners." Both groups pursue technologies to live longer; immortalists hope never to die. In Silicon Valley, these startups are as ubiquitous as high-end hoodies. United Therapeutics aims to grow new organs from human DNA. Verily, a life sciences firm owned by Alphabet, Google's parent company, aims to give people just a few more years. Unity Biotechnology, backed by investors including Jeff Bezos and Peter Thiel, aims to develop drugs that target "senescent cells—cells that, as they age, start producing a colorless odorless, noxious goo called SASP, which Unity's researchers call 'the zombie toxin.'"[3] Calico (California Life Company), launched by Google in 2013 with a billion dollars in funding, pursues a secretive agenda, but in its public-facing work tracks mice from birth to death to identify biomarkers of aging.[4]

Oh, and young blood transfusions? No longer merely fodder for bad teen vampire novels. Alkahest is an industry standard, and targets "neurodegenerative and age-related diseases with transformative therapies derived from a deep understanding of the plasma proteome in aging and disease."[5] Competitor companies pitch their services even more boldly: if you were born before 1991 and live in the United States, the company Ambrosia will ship you a liter of healthy, young blood for $5500. That's just a couple dozen high-end hoodies.[6]

Let's continue our tour, this time to some more familiar locations. Google: the tech giant promises us unprecedented access to human knowledge at the swipe of a screen. Plato, Leonardo da Vinci, generations of high school English teachers: none had access to the information that lies behind your smart phone screen. Facebook, Snapchat, Instagram, Twitter: all provide new modes of social interaction from the privacy of our own homes. And in Seattle, Amazon: capable of locating far-flung items for purchase (a pair of scissors from Japan! A rediscovered Miles Davis tune, *on vinyl!* A book on human enhancement!) and delivering them to your door in two days or less.

We'll end our tour at Stanford University. Here, a less visible kind of revolution is underway. A drug-fueled one. Study drugs, that is: the use of unprescribed medications such as Adderall, Ritalin, and Modafinil by college students hoping for a leg up during finals week. Do they work? Maybe. A recent article by researchers Ruairidh Battleday and Anna-Katherine Brem found that Modafinil—a medication typically used to treat sleep disorders such as apnea and narcolepsy—can marginally boost attention, learning, and memory, though the drug seems to have little effect on creativity.[7] The takeaway: study drugs won't skyrocket you to the Honor's list, but they might help give an edge to your late-night study sessions. More shocking than study drug effectiveness, however, is their widespread use. Study drugs are no niche taste. One survey found of students at a small college found that 35.5 percent of students had used them.[8] Another, more widely distributed survey, found that an average of 6.9 percent of college students had used study drugs, but that usage rates climbed at schools with more cutthroat admission standards.[9] At a competitive place like Stanford, then, you can bet that study drug use is rampant. See those students streaming into the library? Check their backpacks, and you'll likely find some Ziploc bags of unprescribed Adderall or Modafinil, purchased underground in hopes of a top-notch internship or stellar first job. Human enhancement, taken out of the hands of the Valley's executives, and into those of the next generation's ruling class.

All right, folks, tour is over. Grab a bite of sushi from the kiosk over there, post a picture of the experience to social media, and come back again next year. We'll have more innovations, more startups, more ways of making you a better you!

As you saunter back to your hotel, you gather your thoughts. Surely, you reflect, we live in a brave new world, one in which modern technology serves up new possibilities at each new turn.[10] Life in the 1950s, let alone 1750s? Messy, unpredictable, stale. Life now? Well, at least not *that*. Or at least that's the message we get from tech entrepreneurs. And often, from the broader culture.

How to respond to these promises of perfection? Do you jump at the chance for young blood transfusions, join the ranks of future "Linkers," invite Siri into your life, pursue new followers on social media with reckless abandon? Or do you summarily reject all of it? Ditch the smartphone; decline the promises of a better you; unfriend your roster of social media connections? The questions are not hypothetical, nor fodder for some far-flung future. We rather face these questions daily—whether we acknowledge them or not—and will only face more difficult questions in the months, years, and decades to come. We must carefully reflect on them *now*, before we find ourselves already living out our answers to them.

We needn't embark on the journey alone. As we'll see, a range of scholars, influencers, and everyday Joes have already weighed in on our collective quest for more perfect lives. On one end of the spectrum, we'll encounter the transhumanists, who push us to pursue more, more, MORE. We'll also encounter the modern Luddite, those who, like their technology-smashing forebears, would have us toss modern technology to the curb, getting our heads out of the clouds to focus our attention and lives elsewhere.

Ultimately, however, I won't be casting my lot with either. That's for a couple reasons. First, and as we'll discuss in detail later, there are significant problems with both sides: their downfalls lie in the extreme positions they stake out, positions that can't be maintained in the face of level-headed analysis.

But there's also a second reason that I won't side with the transhumanists or modern Luddite. This reason has less to do with the problems they face, and more to do with the positive view I accept. In what follows, we'll call it the fallen dignity view. The fallen dignity view includes two ideas that may seem to be at odds but can in fact be held in a productive tension: the fundamental dignity of all human beings; and the fact of human fallenness. If some of those ideas are new to you, don't worry. We'll be unpacking them later. Moreover, while these views are based on my own unabashed Christian outlook, don't put the book down if you are not a Christian: the fallen dignity view is widely embraced by non-Christians as well. Plus, I'll be exploring the fallen dignity view not simply as a Christian, but as a Christian *philosopher*. And as a philosopher, I am invested in providing arguments that appeal beyond the boundaries of my own religious community. For now, though, here's the important point: when we start with the fallen dignity view, we gain a foundation for mounting a response to the new technologies and possibilities that are presented to us regularly. And this response, it turns out, provides a middle course between an all-out embrace and wholehearted rejection.

Who is the book for? In short: it is for anyone who is looking for a sure-footed strategy for navigating the kinds of technologies I have introduced above. Want to avoid the all-out technological embrace of the transhumanists and the technological dismissal of the modern Luddites? The fallen dignity view provides a strategy for doing so. Whether you adopt the view because you are a Christian or for other reasons, this book offers a distinctive and level-headed approach to navigating twenty-first-century life. More broadly, it offers a roadmap for avoiding the perils looming in the quest for perfection, even while taking advantage of the tools and resources we have developed for the journey. Our aim: to avoid the hubris of Babel without abandoning what we have learned about tower building.

A few words on how we'll be proceeding. In chapter 1, we'll dive deep into the kinds of technologies I have already introduced in passing. We'll discuss what it might mean to say that these technologies are forms of "human enhancement," and conduct a survey of the possibilities that are presented to us. We'll learn how a zap of electricity might boost your creativity; how shining a flashlight on your brain may hone your intellect; how tweaking human genes could lead to different patterns of human life. Chapter 2 turns from the technologies themselves to the controversy surrounding them. We'll consider more carefully a group we've already met: the transhumanists. In this chapter, we'll scrutinize their vision of humanity—what it can and should be. We'll learn what makes transhumanists tick, explore the appeal of their dream, and see how an undercurrent of this dream runs beneath popular culture. We'll also uncover deep problems with transhumanism. Put broadly: by calling for humans to become more and better, transhumanists neglect the fundamental dignity of human beings *as we are*. Chapter 3 thus turns from the transhumanists to those at the other end of the spectrum: the modern Luddites. As we'll see, the modern Luddites identify several crucial problems with transhumanism, and we should pay careful attention to their criticism. They also, however, often stake out an extreme position, one that, while not morally bankrupt, is difficult to maintain consistently.

We are, therefore, left with no wind our sails, stuck between the empty promises of transhumanism and the overwrought standards of the modern Luddites. Chapters 4 and 5 navigate us out of these doldrums. They present the positive vision of the fallen dignity view. And then they show how this vision presents an alternative to both transhumanism and the modern Luddites. Our goal: an approach to new technologies and possibilities that is characterized by an unabashed commitment both to fundamental human dignity and to human fallenness. Seen from this perspective, new possibilities of modern technology lose the transhumanist luster, but also avoid the Luddite wreckage.

Are you left dizzy by these new possibilities? Skeptical about the newest Silicon Valley craze being worth the hype, yet wary of those who would throw these technologies to the curb? Me too. In what follows, I therefore offer you strategies for evaluating both the possibilities and the limits of human enhancement. A map for navigating the perils of perfection.

Ⅲ

Chapter 1

# New Technologies of Human Enhancement

If you had to pick a hero from a lineup, you wouldn't choose Steve Rogers. A good heart, sure. But his physique? Well, Steve looks like exactly what he is: a skinny artist from the Lower East Side. No leaping tall buildings in a single bound, or even benching his own body weight. Judging by appearances, Steve looks like he would be more at home selling insurance or teaching middle school English or putting in hours as a docent at the local art museum. Not battling bad guys on the pages of Marvel comics.

But of course, that's precisely where Steve shows up: Marvel comics. Steve Rogers, if you didn't know, is the unassuming alias of Captain America. Yes, Captain America: muscle-bound, shield-throwing, Nazi-hunting Captain America. So how do we get from humble Steve to proud Avenger? A bath in gamma radiation? A robotic suit, equipped with weapons and artificial intelligence? Or maybe Steve is covertly divine? Perhaps a Norse god? None of the above. Steve is transported to the pages of Marvel by the Super Soldier Serum, a secret, government-developed drug that boosts his muscle mass, adds inches to his height, and propels him from everyman Steve to superhero Avenger.

Steve Rogers...er, Captain America...presents us with an unambiguous case of human enhancement. Captain

America, Marvel would have us believe, is in every way an enhanced Steve: stronger, taller, more confident, and better able to serve his country. Eventually, I'll be questioning that reaction. The idea that Captain America is an obviously improved version of Steve is founded, I believe, on widespread assumptions about what is good for humans, assumptions that upon reflection start to teeter. Believe that your overall worth is predicated on how much you lift at the gym or how well you can serve society? Captain America for the win. Reject those assumptions, however, and your evaluation will become far less clear.

But we are getting ahead of ourselves. Before we tackle questions about the overall worth of enhanced humans, we need first to understand more clearly what we're talking about. What exactly is human enhancement?

## What is Human Enhancement?

The idea of human enhancement typically conjures an extreme picture: Steve Rogers transforming into Captain America or Bruce Banner morphing into the Hulk. If we don't picture Steve and Bruce, we at least picture Lance Armstrong doping his way through the *Tour de France* or secret labs tweaking human genes to produce designer babies or twenty-second-century cyborgs merging all that's best of humans and machines. Those are indeed examples of human enhancement, and we will discuss each in the pages that follow. But before diving into deep waters, let's test the shallow end. And determine which pool we are swimming in. What exactly do we mean by "human enhancement"?

Scholars disagree. But here's a relatively uncontroversial definition proposed in the *Stanford Encyclopedia of Philosophy* by Eric Juengst and Daniel Moseley: human enhancements are "biomedical interventions that are used to improve human form or functioning beyond what is necessary to restore or sustain health."[1] Note two crucial words: "beyond" and "health." Enhancements do not just restore their subjects to health. They instead take their subjects *beyond* healthy functioning to, well, something else.

Take a simple example: the difference between a pair of glasses and a set of binoculars. Personal disclosure. I have poor eyesight. As in, *horrible* eyesight. When people ask if I'm near- or far-sighted, I respond that technically I'm near-sighted, but I can't see things up close either, so in a way . . . both? Without glasses, I can't drive *or* read a book. With glasses, however, I can see close to 20/20. Glasses restore my vision to a healthy level of functioning. The upshot? My glasses alter my eyesight, but do not count as an enhancement. They restore my eyes to a healthy level of functioning. But they do not take them beyond that level.

Contrast my glasses with a pair of binoculars. My grandpa, a lifelong nature-lover and traveler, bought me my set: a standard-issue pair that brings me six times closer to what I'm looking at. That's not enough for international espionage. But they'll work in a pinch to identify small birds at a distance or watch whales that sans binoculars would be but points on the horizon. Is the boosted vision a superpower? Maybe, though no one at Marvel is going to write me a contract any time soon. Clearly, though, the binoculars do not take my eyesight beyond a healthy level of functioning. They take my eyesight *beyond* a healthy level of functioning. They count as a human enhancement.

A few things to note right away. First, while the topic of human enhancement often tempts us to dive into controversial waters (designer babies! cyborgs!), many human enhancements are unremarkable. Ho-hum, even. My binoculars provide an excellent way to spot wildlife but won't inspire a science fiction mini-series anytime soon. Other human enhancements are even more lackluster. My morning cup of coffee; a heavy winter sweater; a set of well-worn Birkenstocks: all arguably count as human enhancements, since all elevate me beyond merely healthy functioning. Yet none raise moral red flags. One upshot of the banality of enhancement? It is nearly impossible to maintain that enhancements are morally problematic across the board. The morality of human enhancement will need to be more fine-grained than flat-out rejection. We will get to this discussion later.

A second note: whether a technology counts as a human enhancement can vary from person to person and circumstance to circumstance. To see this, we'll take a short detour, through the ancient philosopher Aristotle. Aristotle, in discussing a well-balanced or virtuous life, often brings up a local celebrity: Milo the wrestler.[2] As far as I can tell, Milo occupied a cultural space much like Michael Phelps occupies in ours. An unambiguous athletic legend. And just like Phelps, Milo made headlines for his appetite just as much as for his athletic prowess. According to the official Olympics website, Phelps, during training, consumed upwards of ten thousand calories a day. His breakfast alone was gold-medal: three fried-egg sandwiches (egg, cheese, tomatoes, lettuce, fried onions, mayo); three chocolate-chip pancakes; a five-egg omelet; three sugar-coated slices of French toast; a bowl of grits; and, of course, coffee.[3] Milo, we can assume, ate with equally Olympian vigor. Aristotle, at any rate, brings up Milo's appetite to make a simple but far-reaching point. What counts as a well-balanced life for one person in one set of circumstances would not for another in another set of circumstances. If you or I ate like Milo or Phelps—if we *could* eat like Milo or Phelps—we would be out of commission for a week, not ready to hit the gym. But for Milo and Phelps, ten thousand calories a day is just right. Eating properly is not a matter of "anything goes," but does depend on your context.

What does this have to do with human enhancement? Plenty. For what counts as an enhancement for one person may not count for another. A simple example: hearing aids. Many people use hearing aids to overcome hearing loss, in much the same way that I use my glasses to overcome poor eyesight. Used this way, and in these circumstances, the hearing aid restores health without going beyond that. No enhancement there. Hearing aids, however, can also be used in different ways. For example, I grew up in rural Minnesota, where deer hunters sometimes purchased hearing aids to help detect a soft-footed buck. In this case, the hearing aid takes the user's capacities beyond healthy functioning. The device enhances rather than merely restores. Same technology, yes, but an enhancement in one setting and not in another. The lesson is crucial: we ought not label technologies *themselves* as enhancements. Rather, technologies become enhancements only in those settings where they take us beyond a healthy level of functioning.

## Enhancement in Action

Human enhancement comes in many forms, ranging from the glitzy to the dull. Stream your favorite science fiction series, and you will be presented with the glitzy end of the spectrum: a brain chip that records memories for playback; a platform that lets you upload your consciousness to the cloud and secure immortality; a company that creates intelligent doppelgangers within the world of a video game. That's human enhancement as Hollywood presents it to us. Exciting indeed. Outside Hollywood, however, human enhancements are often downright boring. When I use my binoculars to spot an eagle, that's a form of enhancement, but only a lackluster one. As we examine human enhancement, we'll be discussing both ends of the spectrum: both far-flung possibilities and humdrum everyday technologies.

Mostly, though, we'll be avoiding both Hollywood and your front closet. Instead, we'll be focusing on the labs, tech startups, and medical facilities where new technologies of human enhancement are being developed. These technologies typically fall short of Netflix-ready material, but also present possibilities that go beyond the binoculars hanging by your jacket. Just as importantly for our purposes: they present us with the most pressing ethical questions about human enhancement. After all, unlike your binoculars or futuristic brain chips, new technologies of human enhancement present us with on-the-ground possibilities that we must decide how (or whether) to use. And we must make our decision soon.

## Memory Modification

The movie *Eternal Sunshine of the Spotless Mind* introduces us to Joel (Jim Carey) and Clementine (Kate Winslet), a couple whose romance sours. The bitter taste lingers, but a new technology presents an attractive option: delete the memory of the romance forever. Clementine signs up for the service. Joel follows suit. The technology works for both. But then . . . well, I won't spoil it for you. Let's just say there are . . . complications.

Let's be clear: Joel and Clementine's world is not our world. If your romantic life recently fizzled, sorry to break it to you, but the services depicted in the movie are fictional. Yet not *purely* fictional. In recent years, scientists have discovered new techniques for blunting—if not altogether deleting—painful memories. The secret ingredient: propranolol, a medication widely used to treat high blood pressure. Propranolol, it turns out, not only can keep your blood pressure under control. It can also take the edge off a memory you'd prefer not to have. Consider just a few findings:

In a 1994 study, neurobiologist Larry Cahill and his colleagues dosed people with propranolol before viewing an emotionally charged slide show. Afterwards, these people were less likely to remember details from the show than if they hadn't taken the medication. The researchers' conclusion? Propranolol can effectively prevent people from forming negative memories. The research was a watershed moment. No, we hadn't found a way to reach back in time and tinker with memories. Not yet. But we had discovered a method to select which memories we form.[4]

The Cahill study prompted a flurry of research. Consider one study by psychologist Merel Kindt and her colleagues.[5] Their work proceeded along in three stages:

*Stage 1*

Participants were trained to exhibit fear responses in response to a neutral tone through a process called conditioning. Conditioning is a well-known psychological phenomenon. Most notoriously, by ringing a bell whenever he fed his dogs, Pavlov conditioned them to drool at the sound a bell even when he held back the dog chow. Turns out, we're psychologically similar. Consistently pair two sets of stimuli, and our natural response to one soon pairs with the other. That's what researchers did in Stage 1. They paired images that elicited subtle fear responses (think: startling more readily) with a simple audio tone. Then, they presented these stimuli as a pair. Again. And again. And again. Until a simple B flat elicited the startle reflex on its own.

## Stage 2

After having been successfully conditioned in Stage 1, all subjects were divvied up into two groups. At that point, everyone popped a pill. One group, however, took a sugar pill, while the other got propranolol. The real deal. Of course, no one knew which pill they were getting. The subjects then all listened to the tone again.

## Stage 3

After a waiting period to flush the propranolol, everyone listened to the tone one last time while their fear responses were measured. The result? The subjects who had unknowingly taken propranolol exhibited a diminished startle reflex when compared to the sugar pill swallowers. The conclusion of this study? Propranolol can have a retroactive effect on memory. It can affect our memories *after* they have been formed.

These findings have been well-confirmed by follow up research. I'll mention just one more study. This one was led by Alain Brunet, a researcher who studies the effects of trauma on mental health.[6] For this research, Brunet recruited not just anyone from the street, but rather people who were struggling with a traumatic event from their past. Brunet's subjects each worked with his team to write a script describing the event, and then took either propranolol or a sugar pill. A week later, the recruits returned to the lab, where the script they had prepared was read back to them. As they listened, their physiological responses—responses such as their heart rate—were measured. Their findings? By now, you should be able to guess. Subjects who received propranolol had less extreme reactions to the story. The conclusion? Propranolol may blunt memories to the point that taking the drug can help those who have experienced traumatic memories. And indeed, propranolol has been shown to be an effective treatment for certain kinds of post-traumatic stress disorder.[7]

What to make of all this? Well, not that we have arrived in the world of *Eternal Sunshine of the Spotless Mind.* Our minds are still plenty spotty, thank you very much. Nor does the research reveal for the first time that our memories are fallible. Our memories have always been fickle. In the course of our lives, we lose many memories, amplify others, and mix up one set with another. But here's what's different: we have never been able to do all this at will, with the popping of a pill. What in the past was left to the whims of nature is now, at least in part, under our control. Joel and Clementine, get ready. Here we come.

## Genetic Enhancement

In 2018, scientist He Jiankui announced to the world that he had created the world's first genetically engineered human babies. The twin girls, Lulu and Nana, were engineered by Jiankui to carry CCR5 Δ32, a gene that can confer resistance to HIV. Why? The twins' father was HIV+ and wanted to avoid passing it to his children. The parents' motives, then, were clear enough: to deliver healthy babies. Jiankui's motives also seemed clear enough: to attain scientific notoriety. To be wreathed in laurel, conferred a Nobel Prize, and invited on the late-night talk show circuit.

Needless to say, that's not what happened. Instead of placing his work on a pedestal, scientists and ethicists roundly criticized the research. The ethical issues alone were legion: Jiankui failed to inform the parents about his actions, the risks of the procedure are still largely unknown, and manufacturing Lulu and Nana's genes raises questions about whether *their* consent would be needed to undergo it. Moreover, on a purely medical level, the work is superfluous and misguided: the CCR5 Δ32 gene only *partially* protects its carrier from HIV. And the kicker: Jiankui successfully implanted the gene in only one of the twins anyways. Rather than being served recognition for his efforts, Jiankui served a three-year prison sentence instead.

But the floodgates had been opened. CRISPR-Cas9 had been used on humans. The technology, developed by Jennifer Doudna and Emmanuelle Charpentier, won them a Nobel Prize in 2020. The technology works roughly like this. First, CRISPR-Cas9 locates a gene of interest—it could be anything from the CCR5 Δ32 gene to a gene for human eye color—and "cuts" it, severing the double-stranded helix of DNA. Genes *really* dislike being broken, and so seek to repair themselves. One option: they can patch the break by knitting together the severed halves. The problem: CRISPR-Cas9 hasn't forgotten its target gene, so comes along and cuts it again. Cut. Repair. Cut. Repair. And so on. Until something breaks the cycle.

What can break the cycle? Two possibilities: first, a random mutation could alter the DNA during the patching process. If the mutation is significant, the gene will no longer register as a "gene of interest" to CRISPR-Cas9 and therefore evade its detection system. But of course, we can't control these mutations. That's what it means to call them *random*. They could be anything. But enter a second possibility: instead of evading CRISPR-Cas9 through random mutation, the DNA can instead evade detection by inserting novel genetic material. Picture it as patching a hole in pair of jeans. Sure, you can try stitching up a break, trying to pull together the edges of a hole. But you can also find a patch to cover it. And if you go with the patch, you can pick any material you like. Use a similar swatch of denim or go funky with some paisley.

As it goes with jeans, so it goes with genes. Instead of waiting for random mutations to evade the CRISPR-Cas9 scalpel, the target area can instead be loaded up with "patches," novel bits of genetic material. For example, if CRISPR-Cas9 targets the gene for brown eyes, we could insert gobs of blue eye genes in hopes they get picked as the patch. But note the word "hope." Nothing guarantees the DNA will patch itself with the material we have inserted. A random mutation could occur before the DNA grabs hold of the patch. That would allow it to evade being cut without swapping genes entirely. Or the broken strand of DNA might locate a different patch, latching on to some unexpected piece of genetic material.

Long story short: CRISPR-Cas9 provides an effective path for modifying genes. And it provides an avenue for changing those genes in a way we intend. But it does not ensure that those changes are the ones we intended. That's one of the reasons Jiankui served a prison sentence. The technology carries risks that are difficult to control for.[8]

Yet it also carries incredible possibilities. Already, we have seen CRISPR-Cas9 deployed in the lab to fascinating results. Consider just one example: the human FOXP2 gene is one of many linked to human intelligence. Specifically, it is relevant to the development of human language—problems with the FOXP2 gene can lead to severe speech impediments. Enter a lab that experiments with mice. Scientists wondered what would happen when the mouse FOXP2 gene was swapped with the human version. CRISPR-Cas9 makes that easy to test. So they created a batch of mice carrying the human variety of FOXP2 to compare them with plain old mice. Did the mice start reciting Shakespeare and sign up for debate team?[9] Nothing like that. But they did perform significantly better at maze-running than their unaltered counterparts. Superhuman—that is, supermurine—powers?[10] Not quite. But still. Something new.[11]

What's the endgame of CRISPR-Cas9? In her novel *Oryx and Crake*, Margaret Atwood paints one possibility: a dystopian future of species engineered to meet the fancies of their human creators. Pigoons grow human organs in swine bodies; rakunks blend skunks and racoons to deliver silky and stripy pets with none of the skunk's stinkiness; ChickieNobs (buy a Bucket of Nubbins!) grow chicken meat on an organism engineered to feel no pain and produce meat at twice the rate of standard, pain-hobbled chickens. The list goes on. Once we've started engineering non-human animals, we can bring Atwood's novel to life, letting our creativity run wild.

But of course CRISPR-Cas9 also carries with it the potential for *human* enhancement. Lulu and Nana count as enhanced humans, on the way we are using the term. Captain America they are not, but one of them does carry an advantageous gene, a gene she would not otherwise have carried. And we can imagine other possibilities. Olympians with gorilla genes allowing them to deadlift two thousand pounds. Hollywood actors with built-in cologne, conferred by a mixture of lemon and pine genes. Scholars with chimp genes that provide an uptick in working memory. If there's a gene for it, CRISPR-Cas9 allows us to view it not merely as a naturally occurring shade, but as a hue in our creative palate.

## Cognitive Enhancement

Pop quiz. Take a minute to answer the following questions.

1. What is the name of the fictional racoon/skunk hybrid I described above?
2. What are the first ten digits in the decimal expansion of pi?

3. What is the capitol of South Dakota?
4. What did you eat for breakfast last Wednesday?
5. What is the atomic weight of gold?

Mull on these for a moment. Try not to consult your smartphone. Can you answer a couple?

Okay, I won't belabor the exercise. This quiz: not graded. Here are the answers.

1. Rakunks
2. 3.141592653
3. Pierre
4. I don't know! It would be weird if I did. For me, though, the answer is (almost) always the same: oatmeal.
5. 197

Maybe you answered each question correctly. I wouldn't have. Even if you aced it, however, I could have created a more difficult quiz you would have bombed.

Why do I highlight this? To notch down your self-estimation? Well, maybe a little. After all, philosophers and everyday Joes alike have a long tradition of lauding human intelligence. Of placing our cognitive abilities on a pedestal. We like to think of ourselves as perched at the pinnacle of creation, and of the human IQ as a natural or supernatural grace bestowed upon an otherwise unintelligent world.

Yet a moment's reflection reveals this can't quite be right. The quiz you just took highlights a simple fact: we are not as smart as we sometimes think we are. This idea, in fact, has been a leitmotif of twentieth and twenty-first century scholarship in psychology, which has shown us time and again that our reasoning can be clouded by bias, undermined by irrelevant environmental influences, and led astray by ingrained patterns of thinking. For example, we can be "primed," or nudged in certain behavioral directions by our environments. To take just one astounding example: a human who is primed by a computer background depicting money will be less likely to help someone pick up a set of dropped pencils.[12] Speaking of money, contemporary economics has also had to grapple with the fact that humans, who are often thought to be rational decision-makers, can exhibit deeply flawed thinking. One study, for example, showed that judicial rulings can be affected by whether the judge has taken a recent snack break.[13] Likewise, Nobel-prize winner Daniel Kahneman has shown myriad ways in which humans are bad—*embarrassingly* bad—at statistical reasoning. Sure, humans can use statistics, but Kahneman's research suggests that for most, mastering stats is an uphill battle.[14] Biology, too, has revealed our unmatched intelligence to be, well, *matched*, or even outflanked in certain ways, in the animal kingdom. Chimps, octopi, migratory birds: all exhibit forms of intelligence beyond what we humans can muster. The working memory of chimps stands out. Put simply: don't ever try to play the game Memory with a chimp. The chimp would beat you as quickly as you would checkmate him.[15]

All this might lead you to wonder: wouldn't it be nice if we could be smarter? Just a bit? Maybe then we could inhabit the esteemed position where we already assume ourselves to reside. More immediately, maybe with a little cognitive boost, you could bump up your grade in organic chemistry next semester.

I have good news for you. We're working on the problem. With increasingly regularity, the research community has developed new techniques for ratcheting up human intelligence. No, we haven't developed a miracle drug that leaves you crunching numbers like Einstein. Yet we have made recognizable progress.

Start with a study by researcher Jane Wang and her colleagues at Northwestern University.[16] In the study, Wang's team started by asking participants to complete a simple memory task: pairing random faces with random words. So, for example, you might see my face (or, more likely, the face of some eager Northwestern undergraduate psychology student) paired with the word "chair" (or "hat" or "table" or "piano"). After being presented with several such pairs, you would be asked to recall which face was paired with which name. Dull? Very. But also a standard procedure for testing an aspect of our cognitive lives called associative memory.

Memory thus measured, the researchers used neural imaging to pinpoint each participant's hippocampus, an area of the brain associated with memory. Then, to put it bluntly, they gave the participants a little zap. Nothing dangerous. But a zap nonetheless. The results? Enhanced neural function. More impressively: enhanced associative memory. Participants who received the zap became markedly better at the face-word matching task after a few sessions of electricity-laced study sessions. In short: the zapping enhanced their cognitive abilities.

Zapping our brains can also make us more creative. In 2016, a team led by Georgetown University neuroscientist Adam Green wanted to ratchet up our creative thinking.[17] In this study, participants were tested on their ability to draw analogies. The basic idea: the less obvious the analogies you draw, the more creatively you are engaging with them. For example, complete the following analogy:

As large as _____.

Some obvious (and thus less creative) answers you could give: an elephant; a boulder; the moon. But there are also less obvious (and thus more creative) answers you could provide: the US national debt; Paul Bunyan's appetite; the Beatles' record sales. Okay, I'm not winning the Pulitzer Prize with either set of examples, but you get the point. Less obvious analogies mean more creativity; more obvious analogies mean less creativity. With this task on hand, Green and his team, like Wang's, reached for the wall socket. Zap some brains and see what happens. And the result? Once again: a cognitive boost. A zap to the brain yielded more creative analogies in participants.

Maybe, though, you want a cognitive edge without having to plug anything in. Good news. We've already seen one route. In this book's introduction, I mentioned the prevalence of study drugs on college campuses. But I also mentioned their effectiveness. For example, the drug modafinil has been shown to boost cognitive performance in several tasks.[18] Several drugs—often developed to treat diagnoses such as attention deficit hyperactive disorder (ADHD)—have also turned out to be at least a little effective in boosting cognitive performance. Organic chemistry final, here we come.

## Optogenetics

Light. It provides a clichéd metaphor for taking a step forward: we seek a "lightbulb" moment; an article "illuminates" a new perspective; a lecture "sheds light" on a difficult topic. But light also provides a literal way forward for human enhancement. Consider the field of optogenetics, a technique that allows for the direct stimulation of the brain by—you guessed it—light. Yup, that's right. Power your brain by shining a flashlight on your grey matter.

When I first learned about optogenetics, it sounded too strange to be true. To be honest, had I heard about the technology in a late-night science fiction show, I would have sneered: "The writers could have done better than this. Seriously? Light-powered brains? I mean, come on." But that's not where I heard about optogenetics. Instead, I heard about it in a neuroscience seminar. From a real-life neuroscientist. So instead of dismissing it, I paid careful attention.

The technology takes advantage of the fact that the brain is intricate yet runs on simple processes. Everything the human brain does—from processing the figures in a Renoir masterpiece to storing the multiplication tables you memorized in third grade—comes down to the firing of individual brain cells or neurons. Whether an individual neuron fires, in turn, depends on the chemical and electrical signals it receives from nearby neurons: each neuron excites or inhibits—that is, increases or decreases—the chances that its neighbor will fire. When one neuron fires, that either excites or inhibits its neighbors. Which in turn excites or inhibits its neighbors. Which, in turn. . . . You get the idea. Now, multiply this simple process by the approximately eighty-six *billion* neurons in the human brain, and you get human brain function. The rest, as they say, is details. Important and byzantine details, true. Yet details nonetheless, details that build on simple interactions between individual neurons. End of Neuroscience 101.

It is the simplicity of basic neurological communication that makes optogenetics possible. Here's the trick: scientists figured out how to modify the genes of neurons to make them sensitive to light. By combining neurons with light-sensitive genetic material from microbes, you can produce neurological activity quite literally at the flip of a switch. The application of light thus influences which neurons fire. Which in turn affects which of those neurons' *neighbors* fire. And so on down the list. The main pro of optogenetics: its precision. Optogenetics provides the ability to target specific clusters of neurons for activation. The main con of optogenetics: to activate light-sensitive neurons, you need to literally shine a light on them. But that can be difficult, since they are tucked away in craniums behind skulls. Nothing a probe can't reach, but there are, of course, downsides to inserting probes through skulls.[19]

Needless to say, most optogenetics research is carried out not on humans, but rather in mice that have been genetically modified to carry the relevant genes. But even though the findings have applied to our rodent cousins, the potential for optogenetics borders already on science fiction. The technique has been used to manipulate fear responses,[20] hearing,[21] social interactions,[22] and a legion of other behaviors and responses. Because all brain activity depends on the firing of individual neurons—and because optogenetics allows for the careful control of neuronal activation—the possibilities are limited only by our grasp of the brain and ability to shine light into it.

Are there hurdles to overcome? Absolutely. Yet optogenetics presents a promising avenue for human enhancement.

## Longer Lives

The biblical book of Psalms often provides words of comfort for its readers. Psalm 90 flips that script, reflecting as follows:

> The days of our life are seventy years
> or perhaps eighty, if we are strong;
> even then their span is only toil and trouble,
> they are soon gone, and we fly away. (Ps 90: 10)

Talk about a bummer. And we haven't improved things much since the psalmist penned these words. The National Vital Statistics System (NVSS) puts life expectancy in the US at just over seventy-six years.[23] Today, we can nudge our years past eighty "if we are strong," but the spirit of the reflection remains the same: life gets cut short. Wouldn't it be great to extend it?

The quest for a longer life has long taken center stage in myths and stories. The Fountain of Youth, the Holy Grail, the

Philosopher's Stone: all have carried the promise of a longer or never-ending life. Yet consider the story of Tithonus. Immortal Eos, goddess of the dawn, fell in love with the mortal Tithonus. As time marched along, Tithonus trudged closer to death even as Eos remained forever young. Unable to imagine a life without Tithonus, Eos approached Zeus, requesting eternal life for her lover. Wish granted. Yet Eos requested only eternal life for Tithonus, forgetting to request eternal youth as well. And as it turns out, eternal life sans youth is no fun at all. Tithonus aged: his voice shifted from deep baritone to a high croak; his frame warped and shrunk; his strength diminished to next to nothing. Tithonus because smaller and weaker and, well...*chirpier.* Until, in the end, he became a cicada, croaking in horror at his diminished yet never-ending life.[24]

The lesson: maybe you should think twice about extending your life. Yet the quest for a longer life survived ancient Greece. Today, it is led not on Mount Olympus but rather by the titans of Silicon Valley. Walk through the Valley, throw a smartphone in any direction, and you'll hit some startup promising a longer life than the one you've inherited. And the startups are not all grifters: they've started to identify successful strategies.

The best strategy is also a bit boring: exercise and sleep more; eat less; visit your doctor; eat your carrots; don't smoke cigarettes; drink alcohol in moderation. In short, do all the things your mom told you. Turns out, smokers who eat too much and don't get any sleep die sooner on average than teetotalers who eat their vegetables and enjoy jogging. In our quest for the fountain of youth, it is easy to forget that we have *already* made tremendous strides learning about what makes human lives last longer. True, modern science has not delivered a magic pill that bequeaths an extra decade. But take all the discoveries of modern science—germ theory, vaccination, prenatal care—and then abide by those discoveries, and you'll get that extra decade. And then some. According to one estimate by the United Nations, life expectancy has bumped up twenty-six years since just 1950.[25] Of course, some guidance flip flops. Maybe a cup of wine helps; maybe it hurts (or was it coffee? or maybe a piece of dark chocolate?). One study, for example, found that resveratrol, found in red wine, could provide benefits in a range of organisms.[26] The catch? To get enough resveratrol to do you much good, you would have to drink one hundred to two hundred glasses of wine a day. And last I checked, that's going to have some negative side effects. But the waxing and waning of this fine-grained advice never departs from the general maxim: healthy living leads on average to a longer life. And modern medicine has helped us discern precisely what healthy living looks like. Boring but true.

Also, not much of an *enhancement*. Enhancements, remember, take humans *beyond* a healthy level of functioning. Healthy living and modern medicine may help you avoid cutting your life short, but that's not an enhancement. That's maintenance. Have we made any progress towards *enhancing* the human life span?

An hour on the internet searching for life extension technology will yield a steady stream of hyped-up remedies and recommendations. The problem: the flashiest and easiest-to-locate technologies are almost always dismissed by the scientific community as quackery. Cryonics—that is, freezing human corpses in hopes of future resuscitation—amounts to modern-day snake oil. But you can pay good money to companies such as Alcor and the Cryonics Company to give it a try. Or what about young blood transfusions? Despite the vampiric undertones, the company Ambrosia, named for the nectar consumed by the Greek gods, will sell it to you by the pint. Dig a little deeper, though, and you'll find the scientific community's consensus on these transfusions: charlatanism.

There are, however, less dystopian—though frankly less exciting—routes that do show promise. One route: severe calorie restriction. In mice, severely restricting calorie intake can combat aging.[27] It isn't clear, however, if this would work as well in humans. And I don't know about you, but feeling miserable for a lifetime isn't worth an extra couple years, especially if the technique works only in rodents. Winston Churchill once quipped, "I've taken more out of alcohol more than alcohol has ever taken out of me."[28] I'd say the same thing about donuts, nachos, and pizza. Have these shaved some years off my life? Probably, but I have taken quite a bit out of them, too. The potential presented by calorie restriction has nevertheless spawned a generation of YouTube intermittent fasters relentlessly dialing back calorie intake to achieve peak performance. Not for me. I'll stick to nachos.

Maybe you're like me. Good news: there's hope for us nacho eaters, too. Scientists have been working with a grab bag of other strategies that show potential for extending human life—without starving yourself. A recent article summarizing life extension strategies by researchers Linda Partridge, Matias Fuentealba, and Brian K. Kennedy concludes that:

> After long and laborious studies on the fundamental drivers of the ageing process, numerous small molecules have emerged as candidates to delay human ageing, prevent disease onset and/or progression, and maintain human functional capacity later in life . . . . Although a number of challenges remain, including regulatory hurdles, clinical design questions, incompletely validated biomarkers of human ageing and commercial challenges to bringing the

new interventions to market, it is likely that strong evidence will emerge in the near future for feasible strategies to delay human ageing.[29]

One of the most promising of these strategies is metformin, a drug typically used to treat type 2 diabetes. The drug has been shown to increase the lifespan in the worm C. *elegans* by up to 36 percent.[30] That's no joke, though eternal worms are the stuff of nightmares. The drug, however, has also been associated in humans with a decrease in cancer, chronic kidney and liver disease, depression, and neurodegeneration. Importantly, these effects were seen in the context of diabetes research, so it isn't clear if metformin would have the same beneficial effects in people without diabetes. [31] Still, the results do suggest that metformin could nudge up human life by a few years. We have reason to be optimistic.

Our optimism, however, must be tempered with realism. Are we poised to become modern Methuselahs? Have new technologies presented us with a magic pill, able to increase our lives to two hundred, three hundred, even a thousand years? Easy answer: no. Not even close. Still, modern technologies have paved the way forward for what unambiguously counts as an enhanced human life span. Let's hope Social Security holds out.

### Artificial Intelligence

Log into YouTube. Or refresh the page. Notice what populates in your list of recommended videos. The list won't be random. If you are currently nursing obsessions with vintage guitars and coffee, you'll be fed a video featuring a vintage Les Paul, a review of a new pour over brewer, and a demonstration of an amp that pairs perfectly with a 70s Stratocaster. Likewise, if you have been binging on baking videos, the amps and guitars won't take center stage. Instead, you'll see a new recipe for challah bread, commentary on the latest baking craze, and an overview that promises to show why you are doing *everything* wrong with your stand mixer.

This shouldn't be news to you. Platforms such as YouTube (and Facebook and Twitter and Instagram and Amazon) do not randomly generate content that you may or may not find interesting. They don't take that risk. Instead, these platforms are run by their algorithms, which use data about past preferences to generate recommendations. These algorithms inarguably make our lives easier. Amazon delivers book recommendations that we would never have discovered on our own. YouTube recommends videos I would never search for, yet make my sides hurt from laughing. The algorithm often gets it right.

How do algorithms work? That's a question that would take a long time to answer. Speaking generally, however, algorithms on platforms such as YouTube and Amazon function using machine learning, computer technology that "learns" through experience. The more data you provide a machine learning algorithm, the better it gets at performing the task it was programmed to do. Spend a little time on YouTube, and you'll get some ballpark recommendations. Dive deep on the platform, and the recommendations will become spot on. When you feed data to the algorithm, it digests your preferences, and then tailors your recommendations. That's machine learning in action.

Machine learning is but one technology used in the larger quest for artificial intelligence, or AI. AI is exactly what it sounds like: intelligence (or, at least, something like intelligence) exhibited by human-made machines. It includes technology such YouTube's algorithm. But also self-driving cars, chess-playing robots, and voice-to-text transcription. In the modern world, it is difficult to make it through an hour without bumping into some form of AI. In recent years, AI technology has grown increasingly sophisticated, making headlines in its applications to image creation and text-generating platforms such as ChatGPT. Or consider the robot Sophia (whose name means wisdom—a kind of flex for her creators). To picture Sophia: give Siri the body of a thirty-year-old woman, but with a plastic sheen and a nest of wires for hair. The result is, to be honest, a little creepy. But she looks (more or less) human and can carry on an intelligent conversation. She jokes, winks, smiles, and nods. You wouldn't mistake Sophia for the new student in your chemistry class, but she is capable of mimicking human communication to an uncanny degree. Unlike most who are reading this book, she has appeared on *The Tonight Show* and is a citizen of Saudi Arabia.

Artificial intelligence, in short, is already pervasive in our lives. But does it count as a form a human enhancement? At least some of the time: yes. Recall that enhancements are simply interventions that take humans beyond healthy functioning. Something as simple as binoculars are enhancements because they allow us to see in ways that healthy human eyes cannot. So too, then, Amazon's algorithm and ChatGPT and voice-to-text transcription software count as enhancements because they allow us to search for books and compose text and record words in a way that goes beyond what we could naturally do. If enhancements are simply interventions that take us beyond healthy functioning, then in many of its applications, AI is precisely that.

The enhancing potential of AI becomes especially apparent the more closely we are tethered to it. An author who relies exclusively on speech-to-text software; a driver who cedes control of his Tesla to the car's autopilot; a tourist who trusts his route to Google Maps; a reader whose choices are dictated by Amazon's algorithms: each has given up a certain amount of control, but in doing so, has gained an enhanced ability to write and drive and navigate and select books. Or consider again Neuralink, Elon Musk's brain chip technology that may someday provide an interface between our brains and the internet. A Neuralinker, aided by Muskian algorithms, will no doubt outpace the non-Linker along several metrics: efficiency, speed, and maybe even creativity.

AI, in short, already presents us with myriad opportunities to take ourselves beyond healthy human functioning. Give Silicon Valley a decade or two, and those possibilities will expand exponentially. You needn't befriend Sophia the robot—or even accept that artificial intelligence is really "intelligence"—to see the enhancing potential it presents.

## What to Make of Human Enhancement?

In the movie *Jurassic Park*, entrepreneur John Hammond creates dinosaurs from the DNA of blood found in amber-preserved mosquitos. A stretch? Sure, but it was the 1990s sci-fi. Audiences rolled with it, and things went very well for *Jurassic Park* at the box office. But not for many of the movie's characters. A lawyer gets eaten by a T. *Rex*, a scientist becomes dino chow. In sum: all manner of chaos ensues.

Luckily, the movie features as a protagonist a chaos theorist: Dr. Ian Malcolm. Jeff Goldblum's Dr. Malcolm functions as the ethical center of the movie, issuing warnings before things have gone awry and finger-wagging at the would-be dinosaur showmen. In reprimanding Hammond for his lack of foresight, Malcolm utters one of the film's most quotable lines: "Your scientists were so preoccupied with whether or not they could, they didn't stop to think about whether they should."

When it comes to the technologies of human enhancement, we stand in much the same position as Hammond's scientists. Life in the twenty-first century presents us with a lazy susan of opportunities for ratcheting up human life.

Zap your brain to boost creativity; pop a pill to dull memory; skip a meal to add time to your life: we have developed a legion of techniques for bumping up the good parts of life and nudging down the tedium of everyday human existence. Unlike Hammond's scientists, however, we haven't taken the plunge. We are confident we *can* pursue novel enhancing technologies but haven't yet adopted them. Let's not make the same mistake, then, as Hammond's scientists. Let's pause and reflect on whether we *should* pursue them.

m

Chapter 2

## Humanity+

Meet Nick Bostrom. In a *New Yorker* profile, Raffi Katchadourian describes him as follows:

> He has a boyish countenance and the lean, vital physique of a yoga instructor—though he could never be mistaken for a yoga instructor. His intensity is too untidily contained, evident in his harried gait on the streets outside his office (he does not drive), in his voracious consumption of audiobooks (played at two or three times the normal speed, to maximize efficiency), and his fastidious guarding against illnesses (he avoids handshakes and wipes down silverware beneath a tablecloth). Bostrom can be stubborn about the placement of an office plant or the choice of a font. But when his arguments are challenged he listens attentively, the mechanics of consideration nearly discernible beneath his skin. Then, calmly, quickly, he dispatches a response, one idea interlocked with another.[1]

Bostrom is an Oxford scholar, a professor of philosophy. But he bucks the stereotype. No beard stroking or pipe smoking or tweed jacket wearing here. Bostrom's personality seems better tailored to the startups of Silicon Valley than the thousand-year-old hallways and stuffy etiquette of Oxford.

And maybe Silicon Valley is where Bostrom would prefer to be. For in addition to being a philosophy professor, Bostrom directs the University's Future of Humanity Institute (FHI), "a multidisciplinary research institute at the University of Oxford [that] bring[s] the tools of mathematics, philosophy and social sciences to bear on big-picture questions about humanity and its prospects."[2] FHI funds research and scholars who reflect on the kinds of questions that Silicon Valley leaders are (or should be) asking, questions about where humanity is heading, where we *should* be heading, and the risks along the journey. The Institute has attracted millions of dollars of funding, including some generous checks from Bostrom's chum, Elon Musk. Bostrom's core ideas, we will see, provide a clear (though sometimes qualified) endorsement of human enhancement. When asked how to react the technologies we've been discussing, Bostrum's reaction typically is: full speed ahead. His outlook also has a name: transhumanism.

## What is Transhumanism?

Transhumanism. If the term is new to you it likely conjures some strange (and maybe scary) mental images. Perhaps a Terminator-style cyborg, boasting Austrian accent and mechanical innards. Or maybe you picture something different. Perhaps a six-hundred-year-old quasi-angelic being with perfect skin, sipping champagne while reflecting on the rise and fall of empires she has witnessed. Or maybe you picture something different still: a nerdy programmer channeling the Mark Zuckerberg aesthetic, boasting about the promises of the metaverse or a diet supplement or a new personality pill.

Some of these mental images are not far from the truth. Transhumanism, however, is not so much a unified theory or outlook, so much as it is a cluster of theories, outlooks, and hunches, united in their optimism about technologies of human enhancement. The movement was not hatched in academic journals, but rather, as in his *New Yorker* piece Katchadourian puts it, in a "half-crazy Internet ecosystem." Part of Bostrom's success, in fact, came from taming the ideas that had been percolating in this ecosystem. Bostrom is not so much the founder of transhumanism as he is the movement's domesticated P.R. representative. So while we will focus on Bostrom quite a bit in what follows, don't forget: transhumanism is first and foremost a cultural movement, one whose edges are jagged, central contentions often blurry, and manifestations diverse and wide-ranging.

But first, Bostrom's transhumanism. His vision was articulated in a pair of essays creeping towards classics: "What is Transhumanism?" (1998) and "Transhumanist Values" (2005).[3] In these essays, Bostrom lays out some of the defining characteristics of the movement. It is worth quoting extensively from "Transhumanist Values":

> [Transhumanism] promotes an interdisciplinary approach to understanding and evaluating the opportunities for enhancing the human condition and the human organism opened up by the advancement of technology. Attention is given to both present technologies, like genetic engineering and information technology, and anticipated future ones, such as molecular nanotechnology and artificial intelligence.
>
> The enhancement options being discussed include radical extension of human health-span, eradication of disease, elimination of unnecessary suffering, and augmentation of human intellectual, physical, and

emotional capacities. Other transhumanist themes include space colonization and the possibility of creating superintelligent machines, along with other potential developments that could profoundly alter the human condition. The ambit is not limited to gadgets and medicine, but encompasses also economic, social, institutional designs, cultural development, and psychological skills and techniques.

Transhumanists view human nature as a work-in-progress, a half-baked beginning that we can learn to remold in desirable ways. Current humanity need not be the endpoint of evolution. Transhumanists hope that by responsible use of science, technology, and other rational means we shall eventually manage to become, beings with vastly greater capacities than present human beings have.

In contrast to many other ethical outlooks, which in practice often reflect a reactionary attitude to new technologies, the transhumanist view is guided by an evolving vision to take a more proactive approach to technology policy. This vision, in broad strokes, is to create the opportunity to live much longer and healthier lives, to enhance our memory and other intellectual faculties, to refine our emotional experiences and increase our subjective sense of well-being, and generally to achieve a greater degree of control over our own lives. This affirmation of human potential is offered as an alternative to customary injunctions against playing God, messing with nature, tampering with our human essence, or displaying punishable hubris. . . .

Transhumanism has roots in secular humanist thinking, yet is more radical in that it promotes not only traditional means of improving human nature, such as education and cultural refinement, but also direct application of medicine and technology to overcome some of our basic biological limits.[4]

Notice three ideas.

*Idea 1:* New enhancement technologies will help us become *more human.* In lining up behind this idea, transhumanists aim to contrast their position with the one defended by fellow enhancement cheerleaders, the posthumanists. Posthumanists want to transcend our humanity, to become something else altogether. They want to become *post*-human. Not transhumanists. Transhumanists don't want to eclipse our humanity, but rather hope to become the best version of what we already are. They hope to become more fully human.

*Idea 2:* Some people have qualms about human enhancement. Perhaps you think human enhancement is playing God, or that it undermines human nature, or that it detracts from an authentic human life? We'll be covering each of these ideas in chapter 3. Each idea has legs. But transhumanists aren't buying any of it. Bring on the genetic enhancement and brain stimulation.

*Idea 3:* Transhumanists are optimists. Why pursue genetic enhancement, artificial intelligence, and other new enhancement technologies? Because human life is good and could be even better. In this belief, transhumanists may not be very different from your average Joe on the street (at least if your average Joe has a sunny disposition). Transhumanists simply stand out from these ordinary folks in elevating novel technologies as the preferred vehicle for their optimism.

## Transhumanism in the Streets

Transhumanism finds its clearest endorsement in the academic articles of Bostrom and buddies. But transhumanism is not in the first place an academic discipline. The movement is more at home on internet forums than in academic conference halls. I have met some card-carrying transhumanists, but as a professional philosopher, I run in some eccentric circles. Unless you mingle with similar crowds, you have probably never have met a self-identified transhumanist. Nevertheless: I guarantee you have stumbled on their ideas. And that's true even if you don't spend your time scrolling Reddit. The transhumanist outlook is rampant in popular culture, even if it doesn't always get labeled that way. Let's consider just a few examples.

### Virtual Worlds

The Oculus virtual reality (VR) headset hit the market in March 2016. It joined a list of predecessors that aimed to augment experiences (Google Glass! Pokémon Go!) or to immerse us entirely in virtual worlds (VR kiosks at the mall!). With Oculus and its cousins, however, VR experiences have gone from cheesy 360-degree movies marketed to tweens to something truly remarkable. In his book *Reality+*, the philosopher David Chalmers ticks off a list of VR experiences:

> I've fought off assassins. I've flown like a bird. I've traveled to Mars. I've looked a human brain from the inside, with neurons all around me. I've stood on a plank stretched over a canyon—terrified, though I knew perfectly well that if I were to step off, I'd step onto a nonvirtual floor just below the plank.[5]

After reading Chalmers' description, I was hooked. I went out and bought an Oculus for myself. They are relatively expensive, but not completely inaccessible—about the cost of a gaming console. After bringing it home I have had some of the same experiences as Chalmers. And others besides. I have played virtual paintball with a group of strangers, met up with a friend in my virtual "dorm room," and slashed at flying boxes in the hit game *Beat Saber*. Maybe you have had similar experiences. Or maybe my descriptions do for you the same thing that Chalmers's did for me—tempt you to try VR for yourself. This very desire, however, already reflects transhumanist values. Transhumanism claims modern technologies can build on human life to make it *more*. More interesting. More intelligent. More colorful. More human. But of course this list could be copy-pasted into a marketing document for Oculus. VR is what happens when transhumanist values meet the urge to play *Call of Duty*.

## Science . . . Fictionalized

Science fiction regularly asks its audience to reflect on transhumanist themes. Take the hit Netflix show *Black Mirror*. In one episode, people implant memory-recording devices in their brains, allowing them to re-watch scenes from their lives at leisure. Or consider the entire cyberpunk genre—think novels like *Neuromancer*, movies like *Bladerunner*, and video games like *Final Fantasy VII*. Contributions to this genre grapple with themes of technological progress and social decline. Other science fiction novels, movies, TV shows, and video games regularly tackle questions at the intersection of technology, the future, and the human condition. *Altered Carbon*; *The Matrix*; *Ready Player One*; the *Deus Ex* franchise: the list goes on (and on).

Now, if you are a science fiction connoisseur—or even if you are familiar with just a few of the titles I mentioned—you know that most do not provide a ringing endorsement of enhancement technology. Many, in fact, critique transhumanism—science fiction reliably depicts the dark side of technological progress. Yet transhumanists themselves are not uniformly bleary-eyed in the face of new tech. In fact, most realize new technologies come with downsides: they often urge us to reflect on new technologies, scrutinize them for potential abuse, and then . . . pursue them with eyes wide open. And this, it turns out, is precisely what science fiction often helps its audiences do: it helps us explore how technologies can open new possibilities and challenges for human life.

### The Billionaire Space Race

During the COVID-19 pandemic, most of us were sitting at home, trying our hand at baking or bingeing *Tiger King* or worrying out making rent or attending classes on Zoom. But not everyone had that experience. A select group of billionaires had their eyes elsewhere. "Well, if I can't go to a restaurant on a Saturday evening or to Aunt Sherrie's for Thanksgiving, where can I go? Hmm. Oh, I know. How about outer space?" At least that's the pattern of thinking that seemed to be in the water. And the thought led places. To space, specifically. In July 2021, Richard Branson, billionaire founder of Virgin Group, became the first person propelled into space by a self-funded rocket. The same month, Jeff Bezos, former Amazon CEO and (as of the time of this writing) world's richest man, followed suit, launching his fully automated rocket into the atmosphere for a short excursion before it deposited the wayfarers safely back on earth. Easy as an Amazon delivery arriving at your doorstep. Elon Musk, not to be outdone, upped the talk about what might come next: Mars, murmured Musk. Within five years.

What's driving this flurry of activity? In part, to be fair, a genuine sense of wonder and curiosity. Who hasn't dreamed of trekking to space over a long weekend? In my household, the topic comes up frequently—albeit mostly in conversation with my seven-year-old. In addition to genuine wonder and curiosity, however, the billionaire space race is also undeniably fueled by transhumanist values. The transhumanist vision, after all, "is not limited to gadgets and medicine, but encompasses also economic, social, institutional designs, cultural development, and psychological skills and techniques."[6] The billionaire space race is part of the larger transhumanist project of space exploration and colonization to achieve a better (or at least different) life for humans. It's no coincidence that the groups funding modern space exploration overlap with the groups funding life-extension technologies and brain-computer interfaces. On the surface, these pursuits may seem scattered. Under the surface, they are united by a transhumanist impulse.

## Off the Streets and Into Our Lives

What to make of all this? Here's one thing: once we know where to look, we begin to see that contemporary life is shot through with transhumanist values. Wherever we observe the conviction that some new technology will provide us with a new and better life—whether in the push to VR or in a sci fi series or in the billionaire space race—we find transhumanism, even if it isn't labeled that way. Transhumanism is not contained by academic circles or internet forums. Nor is it limited to the self-appointed carnival barkers who sing the movement's praises. Transhumanism is rather all around us. It is part of the twenty-first-century air we breathe.

And, if we are going to be honest, it has made its way *into* us. You may never have heard of transhumanism until diving into this chapter. An Oculus headset may be financially out of reach for you. You may not particularly care what Jeff and Elon and Richard are up to, or where they trek on the weekend. Still: you can't avoid transhumanism. The values and goals endorsed by transhumanists trickle into our everyday, twenty-first century lives—they turn up in our thoughts, desires, and day-to-day decisions. Feel a surge of excitement for a new phone, even though your current phone suits your needs? Prefer texting or social media to live conversations? Use anti-aging cream or Botox or hair dye to shave off a few years? Or plastic surgery to give yourself a new look altogether? Ever tried some newly hyped energy bar or dietary supplement? Ever spent hours immersed in video games on a sunny day? Most everyone would answer "yes" to at least some of these questions. That doesn't make you a transhumanist. Yet the motivation behind your "yes" likely overlaps with transhumanist values. Whenever we adopt new technology in pursuit of a life that is more—more efficient, more colorful, more exciting, more *human*—our mindset is scaffolded on the vision laid out by transhumanism.

Transhumanism, in short, is an outlook that nearly all of us sometimes embrace, even if unknowingly. Where does transhumanism live? In academic journals and internet forums, yes. But more importantly, the movement is sustained by everyday assumptions and values. Transhumanism has left the academy. It has even made its way off the streets. It has lodged itself into our everyday lives.

## Are Transhumanist Values Actually Valuable?

If you have ever lived with a toddler, you have heard the refrain: "Why? Why? Why?" Nearly any interaction can set it off. "You need to brush your teeth before bed," or "the TV has to go off now," or "you need to put on mittens before you play in the snow," or "you should eat some broccoli with your mac 'n' cheese." The refrain can be cute in moderation, and, I'll admit it, refreshing for me as a philosopher, someone whose job largely consists of asking the same question. Yet a little "why?" goes a long way, especially when you are simply trying to get dinner on the table or get the kids out the door to gymnastics.

The toddler's go-to question, however, is precisely the right one to pose to transhumanists. It is, after all, relatively clear *what* transhumanists support. Longer lives; faster technology; more efficient neural processing; space exploration. Exciting? Absolutely. But here's what isn't as clear: what's so valuable about all this? In short: *why?*

A moment's reflection should leave us suspicious of at least some transhumanist goals. Take the goal of a longer life. At first, you might think: who *wouldn't* want a longer life? Life is too short, and sometimes—especially when faced with our own death or that of a loved one—we would do anything to prolong it. Yet we also regularly warn ourselves about the perils of living too long. I remember reading the novel *Tuck Everlasting* as a junior high student and being struck by the horror of the undying Tuck family, cursed with watching childhood friends grow old and die while remaining forever youthful. J.R.R. Tolkien (of *Lord of the Rings* and *Hobbit* fame) puts his finger on the source of the Tucks' horror. He reflects that humans have "a natural span, integral to [our] biological and spiritual nature. This cannot really be increased qualitatively or quantitatively; so that prolongation in time is like stretching a wire out ever tauter, or spreading the butter even thinner—it becomes an intolerable moment."[7] Likewise, Albus Dumbledore, Headmaster of Harry Potter's Hogwarts, observes that when it comes to wanting to live forever, "humans do have a knack of choosing precisely those things that are worst for them."[8] Perhaps the Psalmist uttered the observation about humans living seventy or eighty years not so much out of lament as out of relief.

These observations, though, are more like hunches than arguments. What's wrong *exactly* with living longer? The President's Council on Bioethics—a group of scholars tasked with advising the US President on bioethics issues—helps identify some of the problems. In a discussion titled "Ageless Bodies," they observe that "if we remained at our prime, in full swing, for decade after decade, and perhaps even for a couple of centuries, the character of our attitudes and our activities might well change significantly."[9] The changes, they admit, would not be all bad. Most obviously: "longer-lived individuals would have more time."[10] More time to fall in love, to write a novel, to learn a new instrument, to see the world. On the other hand, the Council worries that a life with no prospect of death on the near horizon could sap our commitment and engagement, as well as our sense of aspiration and urgency. Why wake up early to work on your novel on a Monday if you have a couple hundred years ahead of you? Why visit Tahiti this year if you could next year? Or in a couple decades? Human ambition and accomplishment, they argue, is driven in part by the sense that life does not last forever.

Longer lives would also mean tremendous social changes. For example, imagine competing for a job with someone who has two hundred years of relevant experience. You're not getting an interview. Or reflect on attending a birthday party for your Great-Great-Great-Great-Great Grandma. In one way, it would be a blast. But it would also be miles apart from anything we have experienced. Think it is difficult having a couple generations weigh in on your life decisions? Imagine having a half-dozen generations of ancestors chiming in with their two cents.[11]

The President's Council's observations here are not flat-out arguments against longer lives. Nor do they suggest that there is anything *wrong* with extending the lifespan. Rather, they are observations that should make us think twice about pursuing a significantly longer life. They are observations that suggest a longer life may not, at the end of day, be as obviously valuable or deeply desirable than it initially seems to be. Rather than sinking the project, they take the wind out of its sails.

Many other goals held up by transhumanists face similar problems. A higher IQ; a sharper memory; more efficient neural processing; stronger bodies; space exploration. On initial reflection, these pursuits seem good, even *obviously* valuable. Who wouldn't want to be a little sharper, a little stronger, a little more efficient, a little more interesting? And yet: things that initially seem valuable often come with unforeseen complications and undesirable implications. This is the lesson the Council would have us learn, and it is a lesson we will consider in detail in the next chapter.

For now, consider two things transhumanists can say in response to the concerns we might raise with their agenda. First, they can reassure us that they want to proceed with caution, and with thoughtfulness. Most thoughtful transhumanists do just this. Nick Bostrom, for example, emphasizes the importance of accessibility for transhumanist projects, noting that "the full realization of the core transhumanist value requires that, ideally, everybody should have the opportunity."[12] Likewise, he notes that transhumanist projects carry with them "existential risks," the risk of an "adverse outcome [that] would either annihilate Earth-originating intelligent life or permanently and drastically curtail its potential."[13] Transhumanists should thus emphasize global security while pursuing their projects. Likewise, transhumanists should proceed with "a certain epistemic tentativeness .

. . along with a readiness to continually reassess our assumptions," and never abandon the conviction that "racism, sexism, speciesism, belligerent nationalism and religious intolerance are unacceptable."[14] These cautionary notes do not address all the concerns we may have about human enhancement. But they do safeguard us from some of the most egregious errors that transhumanist projects could fall into.

In addition to tempering cockeyed optimism with the realist's perspective, transhumanists can also remind us that we *already* embrace many enhancement technologies, and that it would be hypocritical to accept these while denying the pursuits transhumanists endorse. Concerned that a transhumanist-hacked lifespan will upend society? Well, then, do you also have a problem with chemotherapy and prenatal care? Both, after all, lengthen human life. Scoff at the injustices of the billionaire space race? I hate to break it to you. The Apollo project was not exactly an equal-opportunity employer. Convinced that a life lived in VR would be inauthentic and unreal? Maybe, but would it be significantly different from the lives many of us already live on the internet and on social media? Put simply, transhumanists can show that while their pet projects may seem frightening, we *already* embrace similar pursuits with open arms. Our preaching is undermined by our practice. The transhumanists train has already left the station.

These transhumanist responses, however, face an important limitation. While they address the question, "why *not* transhumanism?" they do little to answer the question: "*why* transhumanism?" To see the difference, consider an analogy. Suppose I have concocted a new recipe: Peach Curry Surprise. The name leaves you wary. You like peaches, curry, and surprises. But maybe not the three together. So I begin to offer some arguments to convince you to sample a serving:

Remember the allergy profile you took last year? It found that you aren't allergic to peaches, so don't let that worry you. Moreover, I know you don't like boiled things, but I baked this. And the curry powder. I bought it from this cute spice shop on Main Street, the one with the creaky wooden floors and the ancient store owner. He assured me that his product is a fully certified Fair-Trade product. And don't go thinking that I would make you something unhealthy—it isn't! Don't you want to try it now?

These arguments are in one way successful. They successfully address some of the reasons you may give for *not* trying the dish. You now know that Peach Curry Surprise won't make you pack on pounds, that it doesn't contribute excessively to social injustices, and that you won't have an allergic reaction to it. All important things to know. And yet: the arguments likely won't be enough to convince you to try a bite. Why? They haven't done the most important thing. They haven't told you that Peach Curry Surprise is tasty. And, of course, that's what you want to know before trying it—whether the dish is any good.

The arguments in favor of transhumanism we have considered so far have the same limitation as my argument for Peach Curry Surprise. Sure, these arguments may alleviate some concerns we have with transhumanism. They may convince us that transhumanist projects overlap with our everyday pursuits. But the arguments fail to do the most important thing. They fail to show us that the goals pursued by transhumanists are valuable. They do little if anything to address the annoying toddler in each of us, the one asking: "Why? Why? Why?" And in response to this question, we'll see, transhumanists have far less convincing things to say.

## Is A Transhumanist Life Objectively More Valuable?

By now, you should have a good sense of who transhumanists are and what they want. But why presume that what they want is genuinely valuable? That's the question we want answered.

Here's one attempt at an answer. The life envisioned by transhumanists furnishes an objectively better life. On this way of thinking, someone who lives longer, acts quicker, thinks smarter, or jets into space lives a *better life* than someone who dies early, or acts inefficiently, or bombs an IQ test, or never breaks free of the atmosphere. Why engage in life extension and memory enhancement and cognitive boosting and genetic tweaking and space exploration? Because these pursuits will let you live a better life. At least that's one way of defending transhumanism.

I'll admit it: I'm no transhumanist, yet I find something plausible about this line of thinking. There is, after all, something desirable about a life that is longer, more efficient, and more interesting. Sure, we have uncovered problems with transhumanism. Yet if I had the option to gain a few extra years or IQ points or blast into space over the weekend, it would be difficult to turn down the offer.

On reflection, however, it isn't completely clear what it means to say that "a transhumanist life is a better life." In fact, the claim could mean two different things. On the one hand, it could mean that a transhumanist life is more valuable than other kinds of lives. On the other hand, it could mean that a transhumanist life includes objectively good things. Here's the problem: both interpretations have glitches. The first, we'll see, turns out to be deeply problematic. And the second, while less problematic, does little to explain why anyone should pursue transhumanist goals over other worthwhile pursuits. So neither option will do the work transhumanists need it to do—neither will tell us why we should pursue transhumanist projects in the first place. But this is getting ahead of ourselves. Let's consider this line of thinking more carefully.

Reflect first on the idea that a transhumanist life is objectively more valuable than other kinds of lives. The idea, if true, would answer why to pursue transhumanist projects—to live a more valuable life! However, the idea also springs from a deeply problematic assumption: that some human lives are more valuable than others. If accepted, this idea can balloon into downright dystopian thinking. To see this, consider three (completely fictional) human lives:

**Mercedes**: lives the transhumanist dream. She has undergone genetic enhancement, memory modification, and life extension. On weekdays, you'll find her in a swanky Manhattan condo; on the weekends, hobnobbing with celebrities in her sprawling house on Long Island. At eighty-five years old, she looks thirty-five. Next weekend, she'll take her monthly excursion into outer space. Overall, Mercedes is happy.

**Xavier**: lives in small, rural community. He works as a carpenter and spends his weekends camping with his wife and three sons. The job takes a toll on his body (he has a bum shoulder and a bad back), but by his lights, a few aches and pains are worth it. Xavier scoffs at transhumanist projects—give him a day on the lake with his sons anytime over a trip to space or a zap to the brain. And most weeks, he's able to do just that. Overall, Xavier is happy.

**George**: was born with cerebral palsy, and since the age of twenty-five, has lived full-time in his wheelchair. His daily treatments can be painful, and like most people with cerebral palsy, he isn't expected to live a long life. But he enjoys online gaming and has built a community of friends through the internet. Overall, George is happy.

Now, no one will deny that *parts* of Mercedes's life are better than Xavier's and George's. Who wouldn't want a few extra years or sharper memory? Xavier and George, moreover, would no doubt happily swap their aches and pains for a life without them.

Right now, however, we are not considering whether there are *parts* of a transhumanist life that are worthwhile. Rather, we are considering whether a transhumanist life *as a whole* is objectively more valuable than other human lives—specifically, whether Mercedes's life is more valuable than Xavier's or George's. This idea is much less obvious. For if we were to label Mercedes's life as more valuable than Xavier's or George's, this would imply that their lives (and the lives of those like them . . . ahem, you and me) are somehow less valuable than Mercedes's life. That Mercedes's life counts for more than Xavier's or George's. That human value is conferred not by our shared humanity, but rather by individual ability.

This last idea—the idea that value walks hand-in-hand with ability—can be especially nefarious. Some scholars label the idea "ableism." The term is clunky but helpful. Like racism and sexism, ableism divides humans into groups, and then elevates some groups above others. However, instead of divvying up humans along lines of race or gender, ableism latches onto ability. According to ableism, the more someone can do, the more valuable someone is. Ableism, like racism and sexism, undermines the idea that humans share equal value, no matter race or sex or class or ability (or anything else you'd care to list).

In its worst manifestations, ableism can lead to extreme forms of discrimination. Nazi Germany, for example, targeted not only ethnic groups, but also those with disabilities. Likewise, the widespread practice of targeting babies with Down Syndrome for abortion proceeds on rather explicit ableist assumptions. Even in its less extreme forms, however, ableism can have problematic, real-world effects. When we cater to those with influence rather than those who are vulnerable; when we measure our neighbors based on what they can do rather than who they are; when we view disabilities as tanking someone's chances at a valuable life: in all these assumptions and practices, ableism sneaks into our thinking. Stated explicitly, these patterns of thinking are obviously wrong. Yet the seeds of ableist thinking are present in many of our everyday interactions.

Ableism, like other problematic "-isms," thus gets steam from the idea that some humans are more valuable than others. Most of us, I can safely assume, reject this way of thinking. The idea of human equality, in fact, is about as morally basic as you can get. We'll be returning to this idea—and its implications—in later chapters. For now, it is enough to emphasize that ableism, when brought into the open, looks as ugly as its more infamous cousins, racism and sexism. Accept basic human equality? You should reject ableism. It's that obvious.

The upshot: anyone who believes in human equality should therefore also reject the idea that a transhumanist life is objectively more valuable than other kinds of lives. The idea, we have seen, ultimately depends on ableist assumptions. So if you don't want to take on board these assumptions, you can't defend the idea that transhumanist lives are more valuable than others.

Christians have an extra reason to reject ableism. According to Christian teaching, our fundamental value and worth come not from our outward abilities, but from our inherent dignity, a dignity given directly by God. We'll also be exploring this idea in later chapters. For now, put a pin in this: Christianity has no patience with the idea that human value waxes and wanes with ability. For the Christian, human value is God-given. And so, while everyone who believes in human equality should reject ableism, Christians have extra reason to do so. They simply cannot accept the idea that a transhumanist life is more valuable than other lives.

But we have seen that there is a different way of understanding the claim that "a transhumanist life is better than others." Up till now, we have been considering one interpretation: that transhumanist lives *as a whole* are objectively more valuable than other lives. That interpretation comes with problems. But the claim could mean something humbler, and ultimately less perverse. It could mean simply that a transhumanist life includes objectively good things. That there is something good about a long life, space exploration, a high IQ, and razor-sharp memory. That these things are worth pursuing, and that transhumanism's value can be found in pursuing them.

If *this* is how we interpret the idea that "a transhumanist life is better than others," then the idea is much less controversial. In fact, it seems obviously true that an extra fifty years would be good if I want to see the world and need extra time to do so. It seems obviously true that a razor-sharp memory would be good if I want to work at a high-powered law firm. It seems obviously true that space exploration is good if I want to live an interesting life. Are there good sides to transhumanist projects? Yes. And obviously so.

The problem, then, is not that transhumanist goals are bad or unworthy of our attention. The problem is rather that there are many good things in life. And we can't have them all, since choosing to pursue one inevitably closes the door on another. Here's an example: eating cake for every meal would provide me with at least one good. A delicious meal, every meal. But this good thing would come at the expense of others. A healthy diet, for one thing. And my ability to play Ultimate Frisbee and baseball. And the taste of my other favorite meals: chili with cornbread; bibimbap with kimchee; spaghetti with marinara sauce; my wife's lentil curry. If I only ate cake, I would miss out on all these. Admitting that the taste of cake is good, then, doesn't entail that we should pursue it at the expense of other goods. It instead makes sense of why someone would eat cake in the first place.

The same goes for transhumanist projects. Is there something worthwhile about living longer, having a higher IQ, boasting a sharper memory, or jetting into space? Of course there is. If there wasn't, no one would go after them in the first place. Yet pursuing these single-mindedly comes at the expense of other good things. We'll be covering this idea in detail in the next chapter, but for now, it's enough to note that longer lives, sharper memories, and higher IQs may be good, yet attaining these goods often comes with sacrifices. Like a single-minded pursuit of cake-eating, a single-minded pursuit of transhumanist goods can lead to an imbalanced life, one in which some good things are abandoned for the sake of others. The lesson: admitting that transhumanist goals are good is not enough to convince anyone to pursue them instead of others.

So here's where we are left. The idea that "a transhumanist life is better than others" can be understood in at least two ways: we could take it to mean that in certain contexts it is better to think more clearly or to live longer; or we could take it to mean that a transhumanist life is more valuable than others, full stop. The latter interpretation sinks its roots into dystopian soil—it turns on the assumption some human lives are more valuable than others, and that we can determine human value based on human ability. Brought into the open, that idea reeks. Anyone who believes in human equality should reject it. By contrast, the former interpretation—the idea that there are good sides to transhumanists goals—is obviously true. No one can deny that in certain contexts, a longer life and clearer thinking are good things. But admitting this does nothing to get transhumanism off the ground. Admitting something is good, after all, does little to recommend it relative to other good things. Just because eating cake is good in some ways does not mean I should eat it tonight for dinner (maybe I need a meal with more protein) or indeed, eat it at all (maybe I'm trying to shed a few pounds). Likewise, just because transhumanists identify good things doesn't mean I should pursue them at the expense of others, or at all.

When attempting to defend transhumanism with the idea that "a transhumanist life is better than others," we therefore get caught in a dilemma. Interpreted one way, the idea bottoms out in a warped view of human value. Interpreted another, the idea is obviously true, but does little to recommend transhumanism.

Transhumanists—and others similarly enamored with human enhancement—must therefore search elsewhere to defend their projects. And indeed, that's precisely what transhumanists do. Many transhumanists have abandoned the idea that transhumanist goods provide an objectively valuable life. Instead, they lean into a different claim: that transhumanist projects lead to different, more complex, and "higher" goods. But not necessarily better ones. Let's turn to this argument next.

## Transhumanists, Crop Rotators

Recall the toddler's question: "Why? Why? *Why?*" The question can be easy to ask but difficult to answer. I have been arguing that transhumanists find it especially difficult to answer, that they often trip up when asked to explain why we should pursue their vision in the first place. We have seen that the most obvious answer transhumanists can give to the "why?" question—"because transhumanist lives are good!"—bottoms out in either dystopianism or obviousness. So transhumanists find themselves stuck, looking elsewhere for an answer.

Here's one strategy they can take: they can state that transhumanist lives are not necessarily *better* than other kinds of lives. Instead, transhumanism allows us to pursue new and worthwhile goals. Our friend Nick Bostrom, in fact, picks this out as the *core* transhumanist value. He puts it this way: we should pursue human enhancement because it provides "the opportunity to explore the transhuman and posthuman realm."[15] True, monsters may dwell in this realm. But so too may beautiful creatures, creatures we cannot now see, in our limited capacity and vision. As Bostrom puts it, there are "greater values than we can currently fathom."[16] Perhaps these are something altogether new, or perhaps they are "our current values, albeit ones that we have not yet clearly comprehended."[17] Why transhumanism? Because, Bostrum claims, it

> promotes the quest to develop further so that we can explore hitherto inaccessible realms of value. Technological enhancement of human organisms is a means that we ought to pursue to this end. There are limits to how much can be achieved by low-tech means such as education, philosophical contemplation, moral self-scrutiny and other such methods pro-

posed by classical philosophers with perfectionist leanings, including Plato, Aristotle, and Nietzsche, or by means of creating a fairer and better society, as envisioned by social reformists such as Marx or Martin Luther King. This is not to denigrate what we can do with the tools we have today. Yet ultimately, transhumanists hope to go further.[18]

In short: we should pursue transhumanism to discover the new vistas opened by technology, and then to look for and create new experiences and joys and dreams within those vistas. Transhumanists are not wannabe dystopian despots. Rather, like Magellan and Armstrong, they are explorers. Their territory of exploration, however, is not "out there," but rather "in here." The last frontier is not space, as *Star Trek* had it. Rather, it is ourselves.

Let's pause and unpack Bostrom's thinking. The idea, most centrally, is that transhumanist projects—longer lives, higher IQs, sharper memories, and the like—cannot only help us pursue things we already find valuable. These can also open new possibilities that we cannot now comprehend. Why pursue transhumanism? Just wait and see, Bostrom says. Rather than make promises about what transhumanism can offer, Bostrom offers an IOU.

If you're still having difficulty understanding what is written on this IOU, consider an analogy. Suppose you were to try to explain what is great about being human . . . to your dog. Suppose, moreover, that you and your dog could communicate in a way that goes beyond the usual tail wags and ear scratches and playful barking. Your conversation might go something like this:

> *You:* Now Fido, when you are a human, you don't have to abandon the good things about being a dog. But

there is *more* to them. Take food. You know how you like Kibble?

*Your Dog*: Oh, yes.

You: Well, humans get to eat, too. But because humans from different parts of the world have worked on recipes for thousands of years, we have many kinds of food. Thai, Italian, Mexican: sampling all the different kinds of food is a great part about being human.

*Your Dog*: So it is kind of like how we switched from Purina to Kibble last year?

You: Kind of. But it isn't just the differences between ingredients or manufacturers that matter to humans. We also value the cultural dimensions to what we eat. In fact, sometimes we skip the meal and enjoy just learning about different kinds of food. Last year, I went through a food documentary kick. I didn't eat any sub-Saharan cuisine but learned a ton about it. So interesting!

*Your Dog*: Not sure I get it. Take Rover down the street. He gets table scraps. You're saying if I was human, I wouldn't even want the scraps. It would be enough to know that Rover eats them?! Sounds very strange to me.

You: Okay, I'm not sure we are getting anywhere here. Let's try something different. One of the great things about being human is that we have this thing called art.

*Your Dog*: Art?

You: Yes, art. Humans enjoy creating and looking at art. We have many kinds: painting, sculpture, films. One person creates something, and then other people, well, look at it.

Your Dog: So art is just people looking at things?

You: Yeah, I guess so, but not in an ordinary way. Instead, looking at things for enjoyment. Don't you enjoy looking at things sometimes?

Your Dog: Oh, definitely. That's one of my favorite things. So you're saying art is kind of like when I watch that squirrel in the tree for hours at a time?

You: Kind of. But in art, the *meaning* of what we are looking at is usually more important than the actual thing we are looking at.

Your Dog: [blank stare]

We'll stop there. You can imagine how the conversation might continue.

Here's the lesson: it would be exceedingly difficult to explain what makes human life valuable to your dog. Why? Your dog does not have the capacity to understand human values. Sure, it could grasp the basics: humans and dogs, for example, both get kicks out of tasty food and afternoon naps and the feeling of the hot sun on a cool day. But that's about where it stops. A dog can't appreciate modern art or enchiladas or calculus or interior design because it lacks the capacity to understand them.

According to some transhumanists, we may well stand in a similar position to enhanced humans. Enhanced humans, on this way of thinking, will be capable of having experiences and appreciating forms of beauty and meaning that we cannot now fathom. Not that there is anything wrong with us, any more than there is anything wrong with your dog. Instead, we simply are not up to the task of appreciating an enhanced human life. And so, if we were to have a conversation with an enhanced group of humans, it may go much as the conversation with your dog went above. Our enhanced cousins would explain what makes life worthwhile, and we would stand bewildered, unable to comprehend the values of a life that lies beyond us. We would stand in the position as a dog confronted with Mozart: cognitively outmatched, culturally oblivious, and contextually out-of-place.

Why pursue transhumanism? On this line of thinking: for the same reason a dog would aspire to be human. Just as human life is a step up from canine life, so too enhanced human life would be a step up from the ordinary human lives we lead now. And that answers *why* we should pursue transhumanism—to step up our lives.[19]

Initially, this argument may seem attractive. Doesn't an enhanced human life seem *richer* than the lives we live now? Perhaps transhumanist dinners will boast a leap in complexity on par with the leap from Kibble to ratatouille. Or perhaps enhanced human entertainment will differ from our art to the same degree that Marvel movies differ from watching squirrels scurry up trees. I don't know about you, but I'd pay to see what a nine-hundred-year-old, space-traveling human armed with a video camera could put together.

Here, though, we must tread carefully. Bostrom and pals must take care not to slip into saying that enhanced lives are *objectively better* than our current lives. Otherwise, they face the same problems we have already discussed. Say that enhanced human lives are objectively better than ours, and you bottom out in either obviousness or the worst forms of bias. Bostrom therefore makes it clear: "Transhumanism does not require us to say that we should favor posthuman beings over human beings."[20]

But if an enhanced human life is no *better* than the life we live now, why chase after it? Here's what some transhumanists suggest: because such a life would be *different* from the life we live now. It would be more complex, more dynamic, more intelligent. Why pursue transhumanism? For the same reason your dog might enjoy exploring your life. Not because a dog's life is bad. Rather, because a human life offers something different, something more than what a dog's life offers. Same with an enhanced life. It isn't that our current lives are bad. It is rather that an enhanced life offers something different, something *more* than what is offered by our current lives. Why then pursue transhumanism? To discover what is new, what is possible. To boldly go where no one has gone before.

This way of justifying transhumanism avoids the problems we have been discussing up till now. After all, if you affirm human lives are just as valuable as our current lives, you needn't worry about the ableist implications we have examined. Exploring new possibilities simply for the sake of exploring them doesn't trample on the idea of fundamental human equality. So the proposal avoids *that* problem.

The strategy, however, comes with a problem of its own. To pinpoint it, we turn to the nineteenth-century Danish scholar Soren Kierkegaard. Kierkegaard, a philosopher committed to living life meaningfully, scrutinizes the idea of exploration for exploration's sake in his book *Either/ Or*. He labels the strategy "crop rotation."[21] Kierkegaard's idea is this: just as farmers rotate crops, swapping corn for soybeans from year to year, so too people who apply crop rotation to their lives jump from one activity to another. Finish with one pastime, and the rotator moves on to the next. Done with guitar lessons? Move on to podcasting.

Tired of life on Earth? Give space a try. Frustrated by the limits of human memory? Upgrade it in the lab. Someone who practices crop rotation pursues novel activities and hobbies and technologies not because the shiny new thing is better but simply because it is different. Crop rotation thus captures perfectly the transhumanist strategy we are now considering. Pursue enhancement not because it offers something objectively valuable, but simply because it offers something different.

Kierkegaard admits that crop rotation offers some initial thrills. He argues, however, that it is ultimately unsatisfying. There is, after all, only one motivator driving the rotator from one pastime to the next: avoiding boredom. And it may work. For a while. But eventually, the method leads to despair. Kierkegaard imagines a rotation method devotee hitting a wall:

> I can't be bothered. I can't be bothered to ride, the motion is too violent; I can't be bothered to walk, it's strenuous; I can't be bothered to lie down, for either I'd have to stay lying down and that I can't be bothered with, or I'd have to get up again, and I can't be bothered with that either. In short: I just can't be bothered.[22]

We can likewise picture the transhumanist, nine hundred years old and counting, sharp as a tack and at the height of physical prowess, arriving to a similar conclusion:

> I can't be bothered by the new Imax+ movie—too noisy. I can't be bothered by another thirty-course über-dinner—too spicy. Another trip to the moon? Not enough gravity. And don't even mention another UltraMegaMondoMarathon—too long. Truth is, I can't be bothered by *anything*.

Exploration for exploration's sake may offer some superficial kicks. But it won't keep us going. It won't stave off boredom and despair forever. According to Kierkegaard, *that* takes genuine commitment, commitment not just to any old hobby, but rather to a pursuit that is genuinely worthwhile. The very thing the rotator avoids.

The transhumanist idea that we should explore enhancement simply for exploration's sake therefore falls apart on closer inspection. The idea may not collapse into ableism. That's good. Yet it bottoms out in despair. Not exactly a desirable trade-off.

The Christian has further reason to avoid "exploration for exploration's sake." According to Christians, human value is given to us by God. The idea of "exploration for exploration's sake," by contrast, rests on the idea that value is something we find or create for ourselves. Pursue enhancement, transhumanists claim, and you will be astounded at the marvelous things you will find, the new vistas that are revealed, the richness of the life you will uncover. Carve out a new existence for yourself, and you can build up a meaningful life from there. The atheist philosopher Jean-Paul Sartre put the vision this way: "existence precedes essence."[23] That is, first choose what you want to be (e.g., your existence), and who you are (e.g., your essence) will tag along for the ride.

According to Christians, however, Sartre gets this exactly backwards. For the Christian, essence precedes existence. Who we are determines how we should live. The fact that I am a child of God; the fact that God created all humans with inherent dignity; the fact that God has, through Scripture and the lives of the saints, painted a picture what a thriving human life looks like: all these facts determine how I should live and the goals I should pursue. We will be exploring this idea in detail later. For now, note this: *anyone* should be suspicious of the transhumanist idea of "exploration for explorations sake." That's what Kierkegaard's crop rotator suggests. Christians, however, have further reason to be suspicious, and should reject the idea outright.

## Taking a Look in the Mirror

Transhumanists face a problem. Tasked with explaining why we should pursue human enhancement, they must say either that a transhumanist life is better than other lives, or else that a transhumanist life is simply something new. If they opt for the former idea, transhumanists risk falling into ableism. If they opt for latter, despair lurks around the corner. Prejudice or despair. Talk about a rock and a hard place.

It can, however, be easy to throw card-carrying transhumanists under the bus. Those silly transhumanists, we might think. How could they *really believe* that space exploration and boosted memory and better tech could give us more fully human lives? How could they be so foolish as to think that human enhancement presents us with something deeply satisfying? Theorists like Nick Bostrom make easy targets once we have identified transhumanism's problems.

But not so fast. Recall that transhumanism is a cultural phenomenon before it is any scholar's research agenda. Bostrom may therefore be the movement's poster child, but he is not the movement. Transhumanism was percolated in the far reaches of the internet long before it was served in the halls of Oxford.

Moreover: while we can locate endorsements of transhumanism in Bostrom's writings and internet forums, transhumanism is also a pattern of thinking. And this pattern of thinking shows up frequently in our own lives. Whenever we pursue the different, the shiny, the glitzy, or the new simply for the sake of its newness, our pursuit is powered by the assumptions and values of transhumanism. Every time I purchase an unnecessary smartphone upgrade or get caught in the hype of a new tech product release or swap a personal meetup for a digital one: that's transhumanism. When you are tempted to fuel late-night study sessions with ludicrous amounts of coffee; when you seriously consider some new memory-boosting product; when you try a new life hack that promises to extend your life: that's transhumanism. Scoff at the pace of your grandparents' way of living? Transhumanism. Spend the evening immersed in in the metaverse? Transhumanism. Slather yourself in wrinkle-fighting creams? Transhumanism.

Now, mind you, none of these pursuits make you a transhumanist. The point I am making is not that each of us is a transhumanist. Rather, it is that each of us, like it or not, incubates transhumanist values, even if we don't realize it. Transhumanism is not some big, scary, Silicon-Valley-created monster. It is rather a pattern of thinking implicit in modern life, a pattern of thinking that nearly all of us can locate in ourselves. As we have seen, however, it is also a pattern of thinking that is riddled with problems.

So what to do? One strategy is to flip transhumanism on its head. Indeed, according to some scholars who have thought deeply about human enhancement, the proper approach to human enhancement technologies consists not in openly embracing whatever is coming down the pipeline, but rather in running from it. Or at least: adopting an attitude of deep suspicion. That's where we turn next. In the next chapter, we turn to away from transhumanists to those who, in many ways, fall on the other side of the spectrum. We turn to the modern Luddites.

Chapter 3

# Luddism Modernized

The single-season home run record had stood for more than thirty years. Ever since Roger Maris hit sixty-one in 1961—ousting Babe Ruth's previously longstanding record of sixty—no one had hit more. As a baseball nerd growing up in the 1990s, I memorized all the most important stats: most strikeouts, most hits, most single-season hits, and so on. But I never had to revisit the single-season home run record. Maris's place in baseball history stood unchallenged.

Until the 1998 season. Major League Baseball, still recovering from a 1994 players' strike, needed a boost. The race to beat Maris filled the need. Not just one slugger but *two*, Sammy Sosa and Mark McGuire, were on track to dethrone the home run king. Sosa and McGuire appeared in newspapers and late-night TV, their contest sinking deep into the popular consciousness. Major League Baseball fans held their breath, watching as the season's home run counts ticked up towards Maris's record. And up. And up.

Until it broke. Not just once. But twice. Sosa ended the season with sixty-six home runs. McGuire with seventy. Maris's record had fallen.

And the slugging continued. For the next several years, Sosa and McGuire, now joined by Barry Bonds, sent one fastball after another over the back fence. And as they did,

Maris's record-setting season sunk lower and lower in the record books. Today—Aaron Judge having joined McGuire, Bonds, and Sosa in the record books in 2022—the single-season home run record looks like this:

1. Barry Bonds, 73 in 2001.
2. Mark McGuire, 70 in 1998.
3. Sammy Sosa, 66 in 1998.
4. Mark McGuire, 65 in 1999.
5. Sammy Sosa, 64 in 2001.
6. Sammy Sosa, 63 in 1999.
7. Aaron Judge, 62 in 2022.
8. Roger Marris, 61 in 1961.
9. Babe Ruth, 60 in 1927.[1]

The late nineties and early aughts were good years for home run hitting.

But there's an asterisk. And an important one. Ask any baseball fan about home runs during this time, and they will respond with some combination of a wince, a shrug, and a "yeah, obviously impressive, but you know . . ." Why the hedging?

One word: doping. Since Bonds, McGuire, and Sosa set their records, sports writers have spent hours guessing at just *how much* the trio doped their way into the record books. But all agree: at least a little. Mark McGuire, for his part, has openly admitted to using steroids.[2] In 2009, *The New York Times* reported that Sosa had also used performing-enhancing drugs, though Sosa denies it.[3] And Bonds has faced a series of complex troubles turning on questions about *his* steroid use.[4] The records of all three sluggers are now clouded by the suspicion that the home run record was not shattered by natural physical prowess alone.

Hence the asterisk. While no serious baseball fan could doubt the athleticism of all three baseball players, their accomplishments have been undermined by their use of performance-enhancing drugs. This reliance makes their accomplishments seem a little less impressive, a little less authentic, and maybe most importantly, more than a little unfair to Roger Maris. Seventy-three home runs in a season is extraordinary, but would have been *more* extraordinary sans the suspicion that the number was artificially inflated. Performance-enhancing drugs may indeed have enhanced the home run count, but in doing so, deflated our estimation of the players.

As it goes with baseball, so it goes will other forms of enhancement. Or so some argue. As we will see, some argue that the reaction we have to McGuire, Sosa, and Bonds should be mirrored in our reaction to *all* enhancing technologies. This perspective, we'll see, provides a stark contrast to the transhumanists. According to it, enhancing technologies may be superficially flashy, but are ultimately disappointing, and even detract from the goals they initially appear to help us achieve. When faced with their allure, we should respond with a simple "no," the same "no" baseball fans wish McGuire, Sosa, and Bonds would have given years ago. Who are these naysayers of human enhancement? We'll call them the modern Luddites.

## The Modern Luddites

Let me set the scene: early nineteenth-century England. Against the backdrop of the Napoleonic Wars in France and the War of 1812 in America, the harsh conditions at British textile factories threaten the livelihood of skilled workers. Tensions run high. Some workers, fed up, decide to take things into their own hands. Hiding in shadows, they begin to destroy the machines they perceive to be threatening their livelihood. And they give themselves a name: the Luddites. The efforts of the group gain widespread notoriety. They sometimes resort to personal violence, but typically don't go beyond smashing technology. And so the Luddite movement holds steady . . . for a while. But not long. Loom-smashing can fill only so many evenings. Probably more importantly, the British government, through a series of trials coupled with harsh sentences, makes the risks of an evening of technology-smashing seem to outweigh any benefits. The movement fizzles. The Luddites become a footnote in nineteenth-century British history books. They are no more.[5]

Yet the name lives on. Today, in fact, you can acquire the moniker "Luddite" rather easily. You need not smash a loom or chuck a laptop out your office window to earn the label. The term "Luddite" sticks to anyone opposed to a form of modern technology. Today, ditching your smartphone for a flip phone is enough to do the trick.

This chapter, focused on a group we're calling the modern Luddites, will use the term in a more specific way. Rather than capturing *anyone* suspicious of modern technology, we will use it to refer to those who would specifically kick enhancing technology to the curb. The modern Luddites, like their nineteenth-century forebears, believe that certain strands of technology diminish life rather than enhancing it. Why? That's where we turn next.

## Undermining Ourselves

The philosopher, existentialist, and Nobel Prize-winning novelist Jean-Paul Sartre famously criticized a café waiter because "his movement is quick and forward, a little too precise, a little too rapid."[6] Strange, you might think. What's irking Sartre? Simple. The waiter is *trying too hard*. Rather than simply being himself, he is play-acting at being a waiter, and in doing so, living his life inauthentically.

You and I wouldn't be bothered by an inauthentic waiter. We aren't part of twentieth-century Parisian café culture, and so probably wouldn't notice—let alone care about—a waiter whose movements are "a little too precise." But we have all known the kind of person Sartre is describing. And in a different setting, we would be equally annoyed. When a teenager reserves special clothes and high-hold hair gel for nights "on the scene," he is rightly criticized by friends as a *poseur*. When a newly minted high school teacher shows up to class in an oversized tweed jacket with shoulder patches, we think, "Ugh, trying too hard." When a friend adopts a new pattern of speech to make inroads in a social circle, we think, "just be yourself!" All are versions of people we have observed. If we're honest, several may be versions of people we have been. All are versions of Sartre's waiter. The problem: they are living *inauthentically*.

The phenomenon of inauthenticity captures a crucial line of criticism introduced by the modern Luddites. One problem with technologies of enhancement, modern Luddites claim, is that they undermine our ability to live authentic lives. They render us *poseurs*, acting out the lives we desire to live rather than leaning into the life that has been handed to us. This is part of the problem with Sosa, McGuire, and Bonds. Sure, their accomplishments were impressive, but not fully theirs. Their reliance on performing-enhancing drugs leaves us wondering, "Could they have done it *on their own?*"

Likewise, suppose you were to pursue some of the enhancing technologies discussed in chapter 1. Maybe you take a zap to the brain—or perhaps your parents pursue genetic enhancement—to nudge up your SAT score. And suppose the technique works. Your rock the SAT, and the college acceptances start rolling in. Between the celebrations, might you not pause and wonder: "Are they accepting *me*? Or the enhanced version of me? Are these accomplishments *my own*?"

Intuitively, we applaud authenticity and look down on inauthenticity. But what's wrong *precisely* with inauthenticity? Sartre's pet theory: inauthenticity is a kind of "bad faith."[7] Bad faith, according to Sartre, consists in denying the fact of our own freedom. We are free to make our own choices, and inauthentic living covers up that freedom. For example, when I dress a certain way "because I should"; when I adopt a pattern of talking to sound smarter or wealthier; and yes, when I merely playact the conventions of being a good waiter, I take the easy way out, opting for a set of norms that has been handed to me rather than forging a path myself.

For others, the problem of authenticity might be cashed out differently. Consider the idea of your true self. According to this idea—as I have described it in an academic article— "[E]ach of us has a core set of features that are definitive of who we are and that make us recognizable to ourselves and others. Some of these features are products of our own choices (say, my cultivated love of science fiction); others are not (say, my naturally curious disposition)."[8] Your true self, in other words, consists in the central features that make you who you are. According to one way of understanding authenticity, then, "Authentic actions are . . . actions that remain faithful to these features, while inauthentic actions are actions that betray them."[9] When I embrace my love of fantasy novels I act authentically, since that love is part of my true self. But when I gloss over my love of the genre (maybe I am at a fancy party and fantasy is just *too nerdy*), I act inauthentically, since I have denied my true self.

A Christian may identify still different problems with inauthenticity. For example, Jesus' second great commandment—to love others as oneself—implies a love of self (see Mark 12: 31). I can't love others *as myself*, after all, if I don't love myself in the first place. Just like anyone else, however, I fail to love myself if I am dishonest with myself about who I am. For a Christian, inauthentic living thus undermines my ability to love myself and others. And in doing so, it risks undermining the Christian life.

But you may wonder: isn't this taking authenticity too seriously? Are there not occasions in which inauthenticity is not only more appropriate, but perhaps even required? I may feel most like myself in a pair of gym shorts and a t-shirt, but I had better don a tux if I am best man at my brother's wedding. Sure, the tux may feel inauthentic, but if I were to complain about that, you would (rightly) retort, "Tough luck, not your wedding." Likewise, if Sartre's waiter is new to job—and if he is, let's imagine, a bit of a slob—is it not best that he set aside that authentic self and playact the part of a waiter? At least until he gets the hang of it?[10] Authenticity is typically a good thing. No doubt about that. Yet our endorsement of it should be qualified.

Still, most of us recognize thoroughly inauthentic living as something we want to avoid. We appreciate it when others live authentically and hope to pursue such a life ourselves. Despite the nuances in the value of authenticity, the fact that that enhancement can undermine it—can lead us to question the extent to which an enhanced life is really *our own* life—should therefore lead us to be suspicious of enhancement. Or so modern Luddites argue.

## Disrupting Ourselves

Time for a true confession. There are things I don't like about myself, and I would consider changing them, if I could. Here is an incomplete list:

- Like many who work in academia, schmoozing is not my strong suit. At parties, I never know where to put my hands, how to break into (or more importantly, *out of*) a conversation circle, how to read the room. Thankfully, I don't attend many large parties. My social life consists mostly in small get-togethers. But like most everyone, I do find myself at a few social hours or wedding receptions or uncomfortably massive birthday parties. Enhanced social skills would sure be handy.

- My memory is horrible. I have crafted some work-arounds. Lots of lists, post-it notes, email reminders, and calendar invitations. Using these props, I can manage to meet deadlines. But it would be so *much* easier not to have to use them. If only a memory-modifying enhancement could help me out.

- I can't bench press my own body weight. In high school, I would make the attempt monthly. After weeks of practice, I would carefully add the extra weight to the bar. And try. And fail. And repeat. Up until today. I can't *quite* bench my body weight. Maybe what I really need is an artificial nudge.

- My eyesight, as I have mentioned, is horrible. What if I could not only restore my vision, but make it something truly remarkable? So that I could not only pass the eye exam, but make out the tiniest letters on it? Given the decades of blurry vision, it would only be fair. Right?

- I dabble in guitar. Nothing too serious. I strum some chords here, memorize some arpeggios there. But a minute on YouTube confirms how much I need to learn. Compare my dabbling with a YouTube guitarist, and the difference is stark—like comparing Bobby Flay's kitchen skills with a college student's mac 'n' cheese game. Wouldn't it be great if I could bypass the hours it would take to gain the skills of YouTube guitarists? A little enhanced creativity would go a long way.

Each of these interventions—enhanced social skills, modified memory, enhanced strength and eyesight, boosted creativity—would count as an enhancement. Each would take some aspect of me beyond healthy functioning. Most of them, moreover, are not purely speculative. As we saw in chapter 1, we already have developed technology to modify memory, boost creativity, alter psychology, and edit genes to tweak pretty much anything else. Give it a few years, and my wish list may not seem so unrealistic.

So fast forward a decade, and suppose I pursue the plan. Every. Single. Part. Since the new version of me will be enhanced, we will call him Joe+ to keep things straight. Let's compare.

| Joe | Joe+ |
|---|---|
| Socially awkward | Social rock star |
| Forgetful | Mind like a steel trap |
| Can't bench body weight | Throwing up 300 lbs. on a bad day |
| Glasses required | 20/5 vision |
| Guitar dabbler | YouTube sensation |

Compare Joe and Joe+. That's what I am doing. And I'll be honest. I'm not sure I like this Joe+ character. He seems a little too good, a little too polished. He might be a jerk. Perhaps even more importantly, I don't recognize Joe+ *as me*. Even if it turns out that Joe+ is a decent guy, it would be nearly impossible for me to think about him as a new and improved version *of me*. Instead, it seems that Joe+ is someone else altogether.

What does this exercise show? Here's one thing: it suggests that sometimes, the things we dislike about ourselves turn out to be crucial aspects of who we are. I challenge you to complete the same exercise as I just did. Make a list of things you don't like about yourself. Then suppose you flip a switch (or pop a pill) and voila! Everything has changed. When I completed the exercise, I didn't like what I saw. I bet you wouldn't either. The exercise thus suggests that sometimes the characteristics we would initially like to let go are in fact central to who we are. Enhancement, in offering the possibility to discard those characteristics, endangers our self-understanding and our sense of self.

Modern Luddites might put this point slightly differently: enhancement threatens to undermine our identity. For example, in 2003, The President's Council on Bioethics—the group of presidential advisors we met in the previous chapter—published a report called *Beyond Therapy*. In this report, they articulate a perspective that could be described as that of a modern Luddite. For example, here is how they describe the point we have been making about identity:

> With biotechnical interventions that skip the realm of intelligible meaning, we cannot really own the transformation nor can we experience them as genuinely ours. And we will be at a loss to attest whether the resulting conditions and activities of our bodies and our minds are, in the fullest sense, our own as human. . . . As the power to transform our native powers increases, both in magnitude and refinement, so does the possibility for "self-alienation"—for losing, confounding, or abandoning our identity. I may get better, stronger, and happier—but I know not how. I am no longer the agent of self-transformation, but a passive patient of transforming powers. . . . "Personal achievements" impersonally achieved are not truly the achievements

of persons. That I can use a calculator to do my arithmetic does not make *me* a knower of arithmetic; if computer chips in my brain were to "download" a textbook of physics, would that make *me* a knower of physics?. . . In the deepest sense, to have an identity is to have limits. . . We seek to be happy—to achieve, perform, take pleasure in our experiences, and catch the admiring eye of a beloved. But we do not, at least self-consciously, seek such happiness at the cost of losing our real identity.[11]

The problem with becoming Joe+, in short, is not that Joe+ is less happy than Joe. It is rather that he isn't recognizable as me anymore. To gain Joe+ is to lose Joe, and that provides reason to be suspicious of the project from the beginning.

Modern Luddites need not dwell on hypotheticals like this to hammer home their point. We have good reason to think the kinds of techniques being developed for human enhancement can undermine our sense of identity and a unified life. Consider recent research on deep brain stimulation (DBS), a neurological technique that sends an electrical pulse directly to the brain. DBS is widely used to alleviate tremors among people with Parkinson's Disease, can be used to treat depression, and suggests new ways forward for human enhancement. The technique can be highly effective but has a strange side effect—the feeling of being disassociated from oneself. According to one user, being treated with DBS for depression:

I've begun to wonder what's me and what's the depression, and what's the stimulator. . . .There are three things—there's me, as I was, or think I was; and there's the depression, and then there's depression AND the device and, it, it blurs to the point where I'm not sure, frankly, who I am.[12]

If DBS can have these effects when used as a treatment for depression, how much more might it have this effect if used as an enhancement? How much might further reaching and more radical interventions undermine our sense of identity? Interventions aimed at improving some aspect of our lives can, easily and in unpredictable ways, affect the way we understand ourselves.

The DBS and Joe+ cases thus point to a similar problem, one emphasized by modern Luddites. Enhancement technologies, tempting though they are, threaten to undermine our self-understanding and even our very identities. Of course, sometimes a modified identity may be a good thing. If I'm an unrelenting jerk and an enhancement has the unintended side effect of taking the edge off my personality, that's probably a good thing. Likewise, as even the President's Council admits, "biomedical technology can restore or preserve a real identity that is slipping away."[13] DBS users who alleviate their depression may regain rather than undermine their sense of self. Still, given the importance of identity and its precariousness, we ought to be cautious about pursuing enhancement. Perhaps, the modern Luddite would add, this precariousness gives us reason to avoid enhancement altogether.

## Playing God

I regularly present lectures and teach courses about human enhancement. In discussion, especially when the conversation focuses on novel techniques such as genetic engineering, someone inevitably raises the objection: "We shouldn't do that. It's playing God." The comment is on target. A quick internet search of "enhancement + playing God" yields dozens of popular headlines and academic articles.

- From ABC News (November 26, 2018): "Genetically edited babies—scientific advancement or playing God?"
- From the CRISPR Journal (February 17, 2020): "The Promise of CRISPR for Human Germline Editing and the Perils of 'Playing God'"
- From CBS News (November 8, 2017): "Playing God: 'We are in the midst of a genetic revolution'"

Clearly, many people harbor the concern that we "play God" when we tinker with novel enhancement technologies.

As a Christian, I share the concern. And modern Luddites do, too. But what precisely might we mean by "playing God"? Initially, it might seem the problem consists in tinkering with nature, or at least with a part of nature that's never been tinkered with before. Human enhancement, one might say, is *unnatural*. Editing genes; zapping brains; doping with steroids to slam home runs: in all these pursuits, the objection goes, we overstep God's role as creator and meddle with things that are off limits. The philosopher Michael Sandel coined the term hyperagency (that is, beyond agency) to describe the problem.[14] In human enhancement, we act unnaturally by going beyond the scope of agency that has been assigned to humans.

There is something to this idea. Large swaths of human folly can be traced to humans failing to stay in our lane. When we cave to basic desires and drives, we fall to the level of lesser creatures. When we overreach, we commit the sin of Adam and Eve by eating fruit not meant for us.

But the idea that tinkering with nature is itself an instance of human overreach cannot be quite right. Tinkering with nature, after all, is something humans have always done. We build bridges; we fly in planes and rocket to the moon; we scoot around in cars and bikes and trains; we develop new kinds of homes and heating implements and agricultural methods and cooking preparations. These are not bad things, nor do they add up to playing God. Tinkering with nature, in fact, is arguably an essential part of human nature.

For the Christian, there is also a theological problem nearby. When we paint tinkering with nature as problematic, this can come with the assumption that God has kept certain spheres of influence to himself, and that any trespassing will be punished severely. The motivation behind this way of thinking is a good one—it seeks to uphold God's sovereignty. On closer inspection, however, the strategy can have the opposite effect. It can diminish God's power. Here's how: when we describe human activity as "trespassing on God's territory," this can make God out to be in competition with us, threatened by the in-roads we have made into his kingdom. God becomes analogous to a jealous king, struggling to hold onto his dominion in the face of opposition. But that's not the way God is, at least as traditionally understood.[15] God is not some jealous competing power whose sovereignty is threated by human meddling. Instead, he is the source of our ability to meddle in the first place. To say that we can offend God by tinkering with nature assumes that we are in competition with God, as if God were just another faction on the War Room map. But God is not just another faction on the map. He is rather the creator of the map itself, along with all the factions on it. Put simply, the idea that playing God offends God's sensibilities by encroaching on his territory can have the effect of undermining rather than preserving God's prerogative.

There are, however, other ways of understanding what we might mean by "playing God." The philosopher and bioethicist Leon Kass offers one direction. To understand Kass's criticism, some context is needed. God, traditionally understood, is both all-powerful and all-knowing: omnipotent and omniscient. Not only does God know everything. That's the omniscient piece. He can also do everything. That's the omnipotent piece.

Now, when we interpret "playing God" as problematically tinkering with nature, we locate our folly in treading on God's omnipotence. On this interpretation, the problem of playing God consists in usurping divine powers. In an article in *The New Atlantis*, however, Kass suggests we rethink this interpretation. According to Kass, sometimes playing God "means not so much usurping God-like powers, but doing so in the absence of God-like knowledge: the mere playing at being God, the hubris of acting with insufficient wisdom."[16] Let's unpack Kass's idea here. In our technological prowess, we have achieved the ability to modify nature in ways we previously could not. We can edit the human genome, shape neural pathways, and extend our lives. There's no problem, according to Kass, with these newfound abilities in themselves. The problem is rather that in these instances, our abilities outstrip our knowledge. We know how to tinker. But we don't know the downstream effects of our tinkering. As Kass would put it, we act "in the absence of God-like knowledge." *That*, according to Kass, is the problem with human enhancement. In pursuing it, we sometimes act as if we had God-like wisdom. But we don't have that. Playing God does not, therefore, consist in meddling with things we shouldn't. It rather consists in occupying a role we cannot fill. It consists in pretending to be something we are not.

Kass's interpretation of "playing God" has several advantages. First, it turns on an obvious observation—we do not know everything. Hard to disagree with that. Even atheists can agree that there is a problem with playing God, if playing God means acting like we know everything.

Second, Kass's diagnosis of the problem with playing God tracks with purely secular criticisms that are often leveled at novel enhancement technologies. Remember He Jiankui, the Chinese scientist who used CRISPR-Cas9 on human twins Lulu and Nana? He never won the awards he envisioned, but rather spent years in prison. Not because he overstepped God's power—the Chinese government does not recognize such a power. Rather, because he acted with insufficient knowledge of what he was doing. Indeed, there is widespread consensus in the scientific community that we do not know enough about certain enhancement technologies to implement them ethically. For example, in the prestigious journal *Nature*, eighteen scientists—including CRISPR-Cas9 co-inventor Emmanuelle Charpentier—called their fellow-scientists to cease and desist carrying out certain kinds of genetic modification, largely due to concerns of the kind raised by Kass. The scientists are worth quoting at length in their own words:

> We call for a global moratorium on all clinical uses of human germline editing — that is, changing heritable DNA (in sperm, eggs or embryos) to make genetically modified children. . . . Although techniques have improved in the past several years, germline editing is not yet safe or effective enough to justify any use in the clinic. . . . Understanding the effect of any proposed genetic enhancement will require extensive study—including of human population genetics and molecular physiology. Even so, substantial uncertainty would probably remain. . . . It will [also] be much harder to predict the effects of completely new genetic instructions—let alone how multiple modifications will interact when they co-occur in future generations. Attempting to reshape the species on the basis of our current state of knowledge would be hubris.[17]

Note carefully the concerns being expressed here. The scientists are not primarily worried that we have overstepped the boundaries of human influence in the world. After all, the scientists regularly use the technology. One of them (Charpentier) won a Nobel Prize for inventing it! No, their concern is not that human enhancement treads on God's omnipotence. Rather, it is that we do not fully understand the technology we have developed. They don't use the phrase, but their concern boils down to this idea: we play God when we charge forward in ignorance, acting as if we understand something that we do not.

An analogy might help further clarify the point I hope to leave with you. Consider Prometheus and Icarus of Greek mythology. The Titan Prometheus, on the one hand, steals fire from the Gods and gives it to mortal humans. He is punished severely for his trespassing. Strapped to a rock, an eagle consumes his liver daily. Because Prometheus is immortal his liver regrows, only to be consumed again the next day by the same eagle. A tough break for Prometheus (and for the eagle). The Promethean picture, however, perfectly captures the idea that we "play God" when we overstep and tinker with nature. Prometheus breaks apart the divine monopoly on fire, and the jealous gods enact their revenge. So too, on this interpretation of playing God, we overstep when we tinker with nature. We, like Prometheus, trespass on divine territory and will be punished accordingly. [18]

We have already seen, however, why this way of thinking can't quite be right. Bishop Robert Barron summarizes the point well:

> In the desperate zero-sum game of classical mythology, human flourishing is an affront to the gods and must be punished. And then there is the Bible. When the true God . . . comes close to creatures, they are

not consumed; rather, they become more beautifully and radiantly themselves, on fire but not burned up. [19]

The God of Christianity, in short, is not a god of Greek mythology. God does not compete with us for territory in creation, and so cannot be resentful when we uncover a new corner of it.

But contrast Prometheus with Icarus. Icarus, with his father Daedalus, fashions wings of wax and feathers. The wings work. Daedalus and Icarus take flight. In his pride, however, Icarus flies too close to the sun. The wax melts, and Icarus plummets to his death. Icarus's folly differs from Promethean overreach. He does not offend the gods by trampling on their territory. The problem is rather that Icarus does not understand the dangers and limitations that accompany his success. Icarus's downfall is not brought on by God's jealousy but rather by his own lack of understanding. He plays God by assuming a God-like capacity to use what he has discovered and a God-like knowledge he simply does not have. The lesson Icarus teaches is therefore the same lesson Kass and the scientists at *Nature* would have us learn: that we play God with new enhancing technologies when our technological prowess outstrips our understanding. When we navigate this territory, therefore, we must proceed with humility, lest like Icarus we fly too close to the sun and crash.

## Strained Relationships

Modern Luddite Wendell Berry, a Kentuckian, wears many hats: novelist, cultural critic, farmer, environmentalist, member of the American Academy of Arts and Sciences. But there's one role he will never occupy: computer owner. In a short and powerful essay published in 1987, titled simply "Why I Am Not Going to Buy a Computer," Berry defends his decision. One of his central reasons is this: a computer, Berry believes, will diminish the relationships that mean most to him. Most crucially, it would scuttle an important dimension of his relationship with his wife:

> My wife types my work on a Royal standard typewriter bought new in 1956 and as good now as it was then. As she types, she sees things that are wrong and marks them with small checks in the margins. She is my best critic because she is the one most familiar with my habitual errors and weaknesses. She also understands, sometimes better than I do, what *ought* to be said. . . .
>
> What would a computer cost me? More money, for one thing, than I can afford, and more than I wish to pay to people whom I do not admire. But the cost would not just be monetary. It is well understood that technological innovation always requires discarding the "old model"—the "old model" in this case being not just our old Royal standard, but my wife, my critic, my closest reader, my fellow worker. Thus (and I think this is typical of present-day technological innovation), what would be superseded would be not only something, but somebody. In order to be technologically up-to-date as a writer, I would have to sacrifice an association that I am dependent upon and that I treasure.[20]

You need not be married or a writer—or own a Royal standard typewriter—to see the point Berry is making. Modern technology often strains, diminishes, or undermines relationships. The internet alone has upended scores of interpersonal connections. Not long ago, it was standard to maintain professional relationships with travel agents, store clerks, and cab drivers. Airline websites, online shopping, and Uber have stymied all those. Social media likewise can swap in-person relationships with more superficial online ones. When I connect with someone over social media rather than over coffee, I have replaced the intimacy and unpredictability of a coffee date with the delineated, corporate-controlled environment of a media platform.

And those are just basic technologies, ones we use every day. Start reflecting on the novel possibilities presented by human enhancement, and Berry's words become amplified from disgruntled observations to dystopian warnings. Imagine, for example, how an artificial cognitive boost might strain your relationship with a calculus tutor. While her facility with integrals once impressed you, these same abilities, post-boost, may seem basic. Likewise, human genetic modification would alter not only our genomes, but the way we relate to our biological ancestors. Sophia's green eyes? Not her grandfather's, but rather a trait chosen on the whim of her parents. Modified memories could likewise alter our relationships with, well, pretty much everyone. Imagine how your relationship with your best friend would change if sore memories from the relationship were blunted, pleasant memories boosted, and some additional memories inserted. A better relationship? Maybe. A different one? No question.

The media theorist Marshall McLuhan makes Berry's same point a different way, deploying the concepts of *extension* and *amputation*.[21] New technologies—especially human enhancements—may indeed extend our lives in new ways. But these extensions, McLuhan warns, often come at the expense of amputating other parts of our lives. A computer may extend an author's capacity to get words on the page but amputate the connection she has cultivated with a good pen and paper. Google Maps may extend our ability to find new locations but amputate our overall navigational abilities. A smartphone full of contacts may extend the numbers I can dial but amputate my ability to remember the phone numbers that matter to me. In short: gaining territory in one place means ceding it in another. And what we cede, Berry would have us see, is often relational. All too often we lose not something but someone.

But wait just a minute, you might be thinking. New technologies may alter our relationships. But sometimes, these changes are for the better. We all have stories about relationships that we have formed or maintained not despite but because of the possibilities of modern technology. Take my friend Mark. I have never met Mark, at least in person, because we have never lived in the same country. Mark lives in Shanghai, China; I live in Chicago, Illinois. Not a cheap plane ticket. And yet, through video chat and email, I have gotten to know Mark well. We have met each other's families, worked on projects, and shared life trials with each other. I consider him a friend, not merely a superficial acquaintance. And guess what? Sans modern technology, our friendship would have never gotten off the ground. No doubt you have similar stories: friends you have made on the internet; relationships you have maintained through social media; family members you have encouraged through your phone's camera.

And if this is the case with technology as it stands now, why not with novel enhancing technologies? Could not a friendship grow deeper through boosted cognitive abilities? Perhaps your role-playing game community could grow closer, if only each of you were just a little sharper. Or perhaps you tanked a friendship with a painful but unintentional comment. Might not this soured relationship have a better chance of restoration if both of you were to blunt the memory?

Berry's warnings about the perils of new technologies are well-taken. Modern technologies—novel enhancing ones and otherwise—can destabilize, modify, or thwart relationships that bring meaning to our lives. We would do well to heed Berry's warnings and reflect on the ways in which a technology may contribute to or detract from our relationships. And yet, it isn't clear that new technologies always have a deleterious effect. At one point, Berry's Royal Standard was cutting-edge technology. And by his own admission, it has fostered rather than undermined his relationship with his wife. The lesson to draw: some new version of the Royal Standard may be coming down the pipeline. And we may miss out if we adopt the modern Luddite perspective unreflectively or without qualification.

## Enhancement is Unjust

Consider, for a moment, two (completely fictional) characters:

Sonia was born to a poor family in a working-class neighborhood. Her life has been rich when it comes to her relationships. But not when it comes to her finances. As long as she can remember, she has lived paycheck to paycheck. Now, married with three children and living in a medium-sized apartment in a medium-sized Midwest city, Sonia and her husband work hard at four jobs between the two of them. They bring in enough money to make rent each month, buy groceries, and purchase some small presents for the kids on Christmas and their birthdays. They are happy, though they do worry regularly about money. They don't have quite enough to cover adequate health insurance; their oldest kid needs some orthodontics work done; they have nothing saved for retirement; their two-bedroom apartment has been feeling cramped for at least two years. And a vacation? Sorry kids, but no trip to Disney World any time soon.

John lives a very different life from Sonia. Born to an influential family and endowed at six months old with a trust fund, John attended prep schools, then an Ivy League university, and to top it off, graduate school at Harvard. After graduation, Harvard's extensive alumni network landed him a job on Wall Street. Always the go-getter, John scurried up the corporate ladder, and soon found himself hobnobbing with the movers and shakers of culture. Just last week, in fact, he attended a dinner with . . . okay, it wouldn't be right to drop names, so let's just say a *very* important politician. As in, one you would know. Of course, John still has his worries: he has a bum knee that gives him trouble; there has been some drama at the office; and he has been dealing with a bout of existential malaise. But he has a vacation to Bora Bora coming up that he figures should help.

These profiles aren't going to win me the Nobel Prize in Literature any time soon. But consider a simple question: based on what you know, is Sonia or John more likely to have access to the kinds of enhancing technologies we have been discussing in this book? To genetic enhancement, life extension techniques, brain stimulators, and the like? The answer is obvious. Given their respective geographic locations, spheres of political influence, and financial resources, John is much more likely than Sonia to have access. Generally, Sonia's and John's stories suggest it is highly unlikely that new enhancing technologies will be distributed haphazardly. The distribution will instead likely proceed along lines of money, influence, and cultural prestige.

We have good data, in fact, showing that resources are *already* unjustly distributed. According to one recent study by the Pew Research Center "the richest 5% of families [in 1989] had 114 times as much wealth as families in the [second poorest group of families], $2.3 million compared with $20,300. By 2016, this ratio had increased to 248."[22] The United States Federal Reserve likewise estimates that as of 2022, the top 1 percent wealthiest Americans hold 31.1 percent of the country's wealth, while the bottom 50 percent hold only 3.2 percent.[23] To paint a more concrete picture, a recent report by Oxfam estimates that the world's eight richest men hold wealth that is equal to that held by the entire poorest half of the world.[24] Now, we can and should explore the causes of these disparities, as well as what (if anything) should be done to address them. For our purposes, the point to make is a simple one: wealth and resources are not distributed evenly. We shouldn't expect enhancement technologies—many of which will be expensive and resource-intensive—to be any different.

And this, modern Luddites argue, should give us pause when considering them. Here's how the President's Council on Bioethics puts the concern:

> The emergence of a biotechnologically improved "aristocracy"—augmenting the already cognitively stratified structure of American society—is indeed a worrisome possibility, and there is nothing in our current way of doing business that works against it. Indeed, unless something new intervenes, it would seem to be a natural outcome of mixing these elements in American society: our existing inequalities in wealth and status, the continued use of free markets to develop and obtain new technologies, and our libertarian attitudes favoring unrestricted personal freedom for all choices in private life.[25]

Enhancing technologies are not launched in a vacuum. They are rather born into social systems in which wealth, prestige, and influence are distributed in sometimes maddingly unjust ways. Enhancement technologies may very well exacerbate these divisions.

Of course, this doesn't speak against enhancement technologies *themselves*. Many resources are distributed unjustly: drinking water, health care, food, education. This is a problem. However, the problem lies in the distribution, not the thing being distributed. The fact that not everyone can turn on a faucet does not mean there is something wrong with drinking a cup of water. Likewise, the fact that enhancement technologies would likely be distributed unevenly does not mean there is something wrong with *them*. It rather means there is something wrong with *us*: with our methods of distribution; with the favoritism we show to those with money and power; with how we have set up society itself, divided between haves and have-nots. Nevertheless, the modern Luddites' point should ring in our ears—given existing disparities, and given the far-reaching effects of enhancing technologies, we ought to tread carefully when considering their deployment.

What kind of injustices might enhancement technologies produce? The TV series *Altered Carbon* presents one possibility. In this series, a person's memories, personality, and consciousness can be uploaded to a "stack," a computer chip implanted into the spinal cord. A person's stack can then be swapped from body to body. For a fee, of course. The wealthiest in society, however, can purchase an upgraded plan: clone your body; store your consciousness remotely; then, hop from clone to clone, achieving something close to immortality. These wealthy few—called "Meths" after the Old Testament's long-lived Methuselah—can extend their lives beyond the humdrum existence of the world's less fortunate lot. Are we heading toward the world of *Altered Carbon*? Likely not, at least not in all its details. Yet we can't ignore the modern Luddite's concern: that enhancement technologies may steer us towards an unjust dystopia.

But not so fast. Is our discussion here being fueled more by our imaginations than actual, on-the-ground realities of new technologies? By one-too-many evenings streaming Netflix, and not enough reflection on the actual history of technological innovation? The philosopher John Harris thinks so. Harris challenges the modern Luddite using a cheeky example. He asks us to consider "synthetic sunshine," that is, light created by fires and lightbulbs:

> Before synthetic sunshine people slept when it was dark and worked in the light of day. With the advent of synthetic sunshine, firelight, candlelight, lamplight, and electrical light, work, including study and other attempts to improve the mind, and indeed social life could continue into and through the night creating competitive pressures and incentives for those able or willing to use them to their advantage. The solution, however, was not to outlaw synthetic sunshine but, perhaps belatedly, to regulate working hours and improve access to the new technology and think hard about how to manage and control pressure.... Should we, or rather our early ancestors, have turned their backs on synthetic sunshine and gone back to sleep ... and said 'thanks but no-thanks'?.... [I]t seems to me, and I hope now to you, that the right response to things that confer significant benefit to humans individually and collectively is not to say "no thanks" but rather "yes please." Of course we must also work hard, tirelessly, and ceaselessly to make sure that the benefits or their effects are as widely and as fairly available as possible.[26]

Harris's point: synthetic sunshine, in its earliest days, was unjustly distributed. The rich had privileged access to Edison's bulbs, not the poor. Yet the appropriate response to this uneven distribution was not to abandon synthetic sunshine altogether, but rather to make it "as widely and as fairly available as possible." And for the most part, we have attained that goal. In most corners of the world, people can turn on a lightbulb after sunset to work or play board games or read a book or eat dessert with friends. And where people lack synthetic sunshine, we would see its introduction as a gain rather than as a loss.

Applied to enhancement technologies, Harris's reflections on synthetic sunshine should temper our pessimism about its distribution. Will these technologies be unjustly distributed? Undoubtedly, yes. And should we be concerned about all forms of injustice? Again, undoubtedly yes. And yet: new technologies have always been unjustly distributed, and that fact has not kept us from deploying them. We adopted synthetic sunshine and didn't land in dystopia. The same, Harris argues, may also be true for new enhancement technologies. The implication? We can recognize with eyes wide open that new enhancement technologies will be unjustly distributed yet avoid the modern Luddites' conclusion. In the past, unjust distribution did not keep us from adopting new technologies. Why should things be any different now?

## The Parity Principle

Harris's observations about synthetic sunshine illuminate[27] the way we think about the just distribution of new technologies. His observations also challenge us to reflect on a more general question: how do novel enhancement technologies differ morally from technologies we have adopted in the past, or from those we use in the present? Synthetic sunshine, Harris reasons, was unjustly distributed. Yet we embraced it. So the fact that novel enhancement technologies will likely be unjustly distributed does not provide us with reason to reject them. To accept synthetic sunshine but reject brain stimulation (or genetic engineering or life extension technology) because of their unjust distribution would be nothing short of hypocritical.

We'll call this pattern of reasoning the parity principle. We could put the principle like this:

The parity principle: two things should be treated as morally equivalent unless we can identify some morally relevant feature that one has and the other lacks.

Put more simply: if you want to say one thing is morally problematic but another is just fine, you must pinpoint some specific difference between the two. And the difference can't be any old difference. It must be a *moral* difference. Otherwise, you should be treating the things as morally equivalent.

The principle works for anything, not just new technologies. Suppose, for example, that your friend Tina goes on a rant: she deems it morally okay to drink beer but not wine. You listen patiently (Tina is a friend) but find her stance puzzling. After all, there are differences between the two drinks. Wine is made with grapes; beer with grain. Wine is red; beer beige. Wine is fancy; beer pedestrian. We could go on. Yet none of these differences seem to be *moral* differences. A drink's color; its composition; its social standing: none seem to be the kind of thing that make something right or wrong. Of course, someone may think it is wrong to ingest intoxicating beverages. But if that's a strike against wine, it is against beer, too. Both drinks are intoxicating. The reason Tina's stance is puzzling is that we cannot see why beer should be allowed but not wine. This is the kind of reasoning that is picked up by the parity principle. If you want to say that two things differ morally, you need to find the reason *why*. And until Tina describes that reason, you'll find her stance puzzling.

Turn to a different kind of example. We believe—and have encoded the belief in law—that murder is morally worse than manslaughter. Initially, this may seem bewildering. The two actions, after all, are remarkably similar. Both involve one person causing another's death. In fact, if you were to witness an act of manslaughter and one of murder, you may not be able to tell the difference. Yet despite their superficial similarity, there is a crucial difference between the actions. Murderers commit crimes intentionally; manslaughterers do so unintentionally. And importantly, we believe intentionality *matters*. We believe it matters in all kinds of contexts: it matters whether my toddler shoved his sister or merely tripped, whether I skipped our coffee date or merely forgot about it, whether I deliberately flouted the board game's rules or whether I did so because I did not yet understand the game. Our thinking about murder and manslaughter therefore meets the challenge posed by the parity principle. The parity principle says that if we treat two things as morally different, we had better find a moral difference between the two. And when it comes to the difference between murder and manslaughter, we have done just that. The main difference between the two—the intentionality behind the action—provides an excellent reason to treat them as morally different actions.

The parity principle may seem innocent enough. I suspect, in fact, it is a basic feature of our everyday moral reasoning. Yet for reasons at which Harris hints, the principle poses a serious challenge to the position carved out by the modern Luddite. Let's back up a little to see why.

The modern Luddites, we have seen, provide a wealth of reasons to be suspicious of new enhancement technologies. These technologies can undermine authenticity, disrupt personal identity, outrun our understanding, strain our relationships, and amplify injustices. That's an intimidating list of issues. But here's the problem: we *already* use technologies and engage in practices that do the same things. And if we don't find these practices morally concerning, then it is puzzling why new enhancing technologies should be problematic. At least that's what the parity principle suggests. Let's consider some examples. First, your smartphone. Or your computer. Or your tablet. Really any device will do. Reflect for a moment on the concerns modern Luddites have identified with enhancement technologies. Then, reflect on whether these same concerns apply to your device. Take the modern Luddite's concern about authenticity, the idea that we ought not pursue novel enhancements because they can rob us of the ownership we have over our actions. Does not the same concern apply to your smartphone? Might I not wonder: when I use my smartphone to navigate a new city, is it really *me* navigating the city? Is my reliance on Google Maps somehow inauthentic? Likewise consider the modern Luddite's concern about playing God, and the problems that come with meddling with things we do not understand. Then pause a moment and reflect: do you really understand much about the mechanics of your smartphone? Or the downstream effects of our collective internet use, adoption of social media, and generally, of living life through our screens? Even if you are a programmer or Silicon Valley executive, an honest answer is "no." No one fully understands the effects of our collective decision to live a large part of our lives on the internet. Likewise, do not our smartphones—as Wendell Berry (who, if you recall, is *not* going to buy a computer, let alone a smartphone) so accurately foresaw—fundamentally alter our relationships? With cab drivers, grocery store clerks, travel agents, and friends from high school? Obviously, they do. The upshot: our devices raise many of the problems highlighted by the modern Luddites. The parity principle, however, suggests that if we don't think these issues give us sufficient reason to jettison our iPhones, then neither do they give us sufficient reason to reject life extension technologies or memory modification or genetic engineering.

Consider a different kind of example, one that lands close to home. Coffee. I'll admit it. I am a coffee addict. Sure, I *could* get through my day without a cup (okay, okay; without several cups). But it wouldn't be pretty. Between raising kids, teaching classes, writing books. . . there simply isn't enough time in the day. I need a jolt every morning and most afternoons to make it through.

Big deal, you're probably thinking. Why should you care about my coffee habit? You probably have the same habit (or know scores of people who do). Nonetheless, the habit is worth a moment's reflection. Why? Because coffee is an enhancement to which many of the modern Luddite's concerns apply. It is, in the first place, inarguably an enhancement. Caffeine makes us sharper and more alert than our uncaffeinated selves. A morning cup of coffee is no mere treatment, something that restores us to healthy functioning. It is also an enhancement, something that takes us *beyond* healthy functioning.

If we place ourselves in right mindset, moreover, something as mundane as coffee also raises many of the concerns highlighted by the modern Luddites. Do my caffeine-fueled writing sessions count genuinely as *mine*, or are they somehow inauthentic, given my reliance on the chemical coursing through my veins? Might not coffee undermine my relationships by allowing me to edit my work on my own rather than needing to rely on the literary efforts of my colleagues and spouse? Might not my coffee habit chip away at my identity? Do I even *know* uncaffeinated Joe anymore? Truth be told—except for a caffeine-free Lent a couple years ago—probably not. And what about justice? Coffee may be cheap and widely available, at least in much of the world. But might it not be giving an extra (and unjust) edge to those parts over those where it is not accessible?

Might not I be perpetuating entrenched injustices every time I brew a pot of Folgers?

I'll be honest. I'm not losing any sleep over these concerns. That's in part because the coffee is keeping me awake. But neither does the habit make me feel morally compromised, and I'm not moved by arguments that suggest I should feel otherwise. In fact, I think I'll grab another cup now.

This attitude matters. If arguments against caffeine are not particularly moving, then neither should similar arguments work against less familiar enhancement technologies. That's the idea at the heart of the parity principle. If caffeine has the power to jostle my identity, bolster my abilities, and alter my relationships, and if I use it anyway, then it would be hypocritical to dismiss enhancing technologies for doing the same thing. The parity principle demands (quite reasonably) that we be consistent in our application of moral principles. If the concerns raised by modern Luddites pose a problem for new enhancing technologies, they are equally problematic wherever they turn up. Problem is, we don't treat them like that, a fact that everyday items like smartphone and coffee drinking bring out.

## The Amish Response and Back Again

Our discussion has left us in a pickle. The modern Luddites present a legion of legitimate concerns about novel enhancement technologies. Should we be concerned with justice, authenticity, identity, and pridefully overstepping our human limitations? No doubt. The modern Luddites grasp crucial moral considerations, and I'll admit to being moved deeply by several of their arguments. If I had to choose between the modern Luddites and transhumanists, I'd side with the Luddites in a heartbeat.

And yet: the parity principle suggests that those of us who sympathize with the Luddites can find ourselves threatened with moral inconsistency. In one breath, paying lip service to the Luddite's concerns; in the next, ignoring these concerns in the ways we live our lives. There are, by my lights, three ways to bring this inconsistency to a resolution. First: reject the moral considerations of the modern Luddites, thereby rejecting the idea that these standards can provide us with a clear metric by which to evaluate novel technologies. Second: double down on the moral standards identified by the modern Luddites. This means taking their concerns about justice, authenticity, identity, and playing God seriously, no matter where these concerns show up. Third: well . . . we're going to save that option for later.

First, then, let's think more carefully about the first strategy: rejecting the moral considerations of the modern Luddites, thereby rejecting the idea that these standards can provide us with a clear metric by which to evaluate novel technologies. Put simply: abandon the position staked out by the modern Luddites in favor of something else. This strategy deftly resolves the inconsistencies we have been discussing. If you scrap the modern Luddite position, there's no need to worry about salvaging it. By my lights, however, this would be too hasty. The modern Luddite position may be difficult to apply consistently. Yet it raises crucial moral considerations: I'm convinced that while navigating new enhancing technologies, we should pay careful attention to issues of justice and authenticity. Of identity and human limitations. Modern Luddites provide an important moral perspective on human enhancement, and we would be foolish to abandon it entirely.

Let's turn then to the second strategy: what might it look like to take the modern Luddites' concerns seriously, no matter where they show up? Some communities do just this. Most notoriously: the Amish. Amish communities reject (or at least drastically limit) the use of modern technology, for reasons that track with Luddite concerns. They drive horse-drawn buggies, not cars. They light their homes with candles, not synthetic sunshine. They make quilts and pies and tables by hand, not with industrial equipment (in fact: I am writing these words on an Amish-made table). They do drink coffee. But well, no one is perfect, right?

Why all these practices? While Amish communities may be sympathetic to many of the concerns raised by modern Luddites, they often point to the ways that modern technologies can erode relationships. The Amish may not be Wendell Berry aficionados but would echo many of the concerns he raises about buying a computer. Modern technologies can chip away at our relationships, undermine local communities, and replace humans with machines. They can lead us away from the kind of lives in community we were intended to live. Better reject these technologies across the board than start down that slippery slope. At least on the Amish way of thinking. The Amish thus provide a living example of what it might look like to take the parity principle seriously, and to live out modern Luddite concerns literally and consistently.

How to respond? One possibility: go join the Amish. Or at least adopt their practices. Call this the Amish response. For those moved by the concerns of the modern Luddites and believe they should be deployed as broadly as possible, the Amish response would certainly bring you closer to moral consistency.

And yet most won't take the Amish response seriously. Why not? One possibility: most of us are not up to its moral demands. Perhaps we are weak-willed in the face of what is obviously a morally superior life? Perhaps, in the Amish way of life, we instantly recognize the way we should be living, and nevertheless bow out? Maybe. My suspicion, however, is that most of us keep on using cars and cell phones and modern plumbing and synthetic sunshine because we recognize something good in them. The Amish response may be more consistent in its application of the standards articulated by modern Luddites. Yet that may not be entirely a problem with us. It may be in part a problem with the standards. Applied rigidly, Luddite standards may move us away from rather than toward a fully flourishing human life.

There are distinctively Christian considerations that support this line of thinking. Creation, the author of Genesis urges, is good, to be embraced rather than rejected (Gn 1). Likewise, in the Gospel of John, Christ says, "I came that they may have life, and have it abundantly" (Jn 10: 10). Of course, we can debate what an abundant life looks like, but it surely does not require outhouses and candlelight. The God of Christianity, we have seen, is traditionally understood not to be concerned with Promethean overreach. God does not compete with us for territory, nor can we steal fire that God has kept burning for himself. God has instead created things good and wants to share them with us. To guard ourselves by rejecting the goods of creation is to misunderstand our role, and God's.

Of course, neither Christians nor anyone else should do anything unreflectively. As with anything, we must exercise our adoption of new technologies thoughtfully. And the modern Luddites provide helpful guidelines for doing so. But recognizing the wisdom of the modern Luddites doesn't mean adopting the Amish response. In a joint statement, St. John Paul II and Bartholomew I of Constantinople said that Christians should "use science and technology in a full and constructive way," not reject it altogether.[28] More forcefully, Pope Benedict XVI said that "Technology enables us to exercise dominion over matter, to reduce risks, to save labor, to improve our conditions of life. It touches the heart of the vocation of human labor: in technology, seen as the product of his genius, man recognizes himself and forges his own humanity."[29] The Christian must exercise caution in the face of modern technology, but caution need not add up to an all-out retreat. Refusing the Amish response may not be merely a symptom of a weak will but may instead be a genuine theological insight.

The Amish response, then, in one way goes too far in its rejection of technology. That's the first problem it faces. But it also doesn't go far enough. That's the second problem it faces.

Here's what I'm getting at. Applied consistently and literally, the modern Luddite position, combined with the parity principle, would demand a life even more austere than that lived by the Amish. Consider how modern Luddite concerns might be applied even to the simple technologies used in Amish communities. Are not buggies and handsaws inevitably distributed unjustly? Does agriculture not detract from the more authentic life lived by hunter-gatherers? And do not even simple technologies—farm equipment, saws, ovens—alter the nature of our relationships with each other and our environments? We can imagine a rural, hunter-gatherer society rejecting the Amish way of life, and doing so for precisely reasons the same reasons that the Amish provide for rejecting twenty-first century American life. The problem with the standards set by the modern Luddites is not that they are misguided, but rather that they are nearly impossible to apply consistently. Technologies new and old inevitably raise the concerns pointed out by the modern Luddites. But to treat these concerns as the final word—and to apply them to our lives consistently—would quickly lead us to adopt a life that is far from a flourishing one. Christ cannot be calling us to *that*.

## Toward a Fuller Picture of a Well-Lived Life

Perhaps the discussion of this chapter has left you frustrated. Frustrated at how difficult it is to apply the moral insights of the modern Luddites consistently. Frustrated at the simple elegance of the parity principle. Frustrated, frankly, *with me* for making things so difficult. If, as I have argued, the modern Luddite's standards are morally sound, yet near impossible to apply consistently, how should we proceed?

Ah, you're forgetting. Above, I hinted that there is a third option for moving forward from the modern Luddite's position. Instead of jettisoning their view entirely, and instead of pursuing a quixotic attempt at applying their standards with perfect consistency, we can instead take what we have learned from the modern Luddites to build a fuller moral picture. One that is built less on black and white moral principles, and more on a vision of what makes human life valuable in the first place. Modern Luddites offer a robust picture of what makes human life valuable, and accurately identify how novel enhancement technologies can detract from that life. And yet: if our outlook focuses so intently on the ills of new technology, it can lose sight of what ultimately makes life valuable. How to overcome this myopia? Back up, focus on what a human life is, and reflect on how to live one well. Do that, and your vision will become clearer: both your vision of how to live and how novel technologies may fit into it.

So that's where we turn now. In particular, we consider a "big picture" view of humanity, a view of life based on a Christian framework, yet capacious enough for non-Christians to embrace. The picture I describe will ultimately share affinities with the modern Luddites . . . and in fact, may arguably get to the heart of the modern Luddite position. More importantly, it will give us what we have been looking for: a solid strategy for navigating human enhancement.

## Chapter 4

# Fallen Dignity

Josef De Veuster entered the world in 1840, the youngest in a family of seven children. Twenty years later, in his homeland of Belgium he joined a religious order—the Fathers of the Sacred Heart of Jesus and Mary—eventually becoming a Catholic priest. Josef, however, did not stay put in Belgium. He wanted to become a missionary and, after a fellow priest had to ditch plans to serve in Hawai'i, Josef volunteered to take his place. In Hawai'i, Josef noticed something disturbing: native Hawaiians had high mortality rates, dying frequently from leprosy. In fact, leprosy (still incurable at the time) was such a problem, Hawaiian King Kamehameha V quarantined anyone diagnosed with it in an isolated colony to contain the spread. Already far from home, Josef volunteered to minister to the lepers in the colony. While others would not touch or even go near someone with leprosy, Josef moved into the settlement: eating with the members of the colony; living with them; smoking pipes with them. In short, sharing life. In 1884, the inevitable happened—he contracted leprosy himself. He died from it five years later.[1]

Anjezë Bojaxhiu was born in Albania in 1910. Like Josef, she was the youngest child in the family. At the age of just eighteen, she joined the Sisters of Loreto in Ireland. Why Ireland rather than her home Albania? She wanted to learn

English so she could become a missionary. A year after joining, she left for India, where she added Bengali to her repertoire of languages and began a career as a teacher. She taught for nearly twenty years—a chunk of time after which most of us would start thinking about retirement. Not Anjezë. Rather than anticipating nights of bridge and bingo, she found herself dissatisfied. How could she stay confined to the relative comfort of her school, ignoring the poverty around her? Eventually, she decided she would leave the convent and her teaching behind. What for? To live on the streets, in the service of "the hungry, of the naked, of the homeless, of the crippled, of the blind, of the leprous, of all those people who felt unwanted, unloved, uncared, thrown away by society, people who have become a burden to the society."[2] And that's just what she did. She lived among and cared for the poorest of the poor in the streets of Calcutta until she died in 1997.[3]

If you didn't recognize the figures, Josef is Saint Damien of Molokai and Anjezë is Saint Mother Teresa of Calcutta. Both modern individuals, they strike us (okay, they strike *me*) as morally praiseworthy, but a touch incomprehensible. While I admire their lives and agree wholeheartedly with their vision, a part of me wonders: who *does* that? Who willingly lives in close quarters with a community suffering from a communicable, incurable, and disfiguring disease? Who abandons a comfortable life as a teacher to live in the street, serving the poorest of the poor? If I'm being honest, not me. Maybe I lack the moral gumption; maybe I'm too tied down with family life; or maybe my vocation lies along a very different path. But for me, at least, figures such as Saints Damien of Molokai and Mother Teresa present a moral ideal that is deeply desirable but near-impossible to picture myself emulating. Frankly, it is difficult to understand in the first place.

In this chapter, I aim to understand it just a little more. More specifically, I aim to diagnose the foundational moral commitments at the heart of the lives of figures such as Damien of Molokai and Mother Teresa. The lives of such figures, I'll suggest, are built upon a foundation of what I'll call the fallen dignity view. The fallen dignity view is based on two beliefs, both unambiguously Christian yet widely endorsed by non-Christians as well. The first: an unwavering commitment to human equality, the idea of the fundamental dignity and worth of every human being. The second: an acceptance of human limitations and fallenness. Both ideas are relatively easy to articulate. Initially, they may even see intuitive. But as we'll see, they morph into something radical if they are lived out consistently, especially in the face of a culture that actively works to undermine them.

The fallen dignity view also provides us with a map for navigating new technologies of human enhancement. Using that map, we can trace a route that takes us toward the advantages of both the modern Luddites and the transhumanists even while avoiding their excesses and problems. My conclusion? The fallen dignity approach to human enhancement offers something different from what we have seen so far. Something distinctive. Something *better*.

That, at any rate, is where we are heading. But before setting out, we need to get clear on the place of our departure. We need to articulate the ideas of dignity, equality, and fallenness on their own terms. That's where we turn now.

## The Basic Equality View

Ancient Romans followed a common practice called infant exposure. After an unwanted baby was born, it was often thrown to the curb and left to die. Infant exposure weeded unwelcome traits from the gene pool and, in an age long before effective artificial contraception, limited family size. Early Christians, however, would have none of it. They scandalized their contemporaries by rescuing abandoned children, bringing them into their fold, and raising them as their own. In short: they not only refused to adopt the practices of their Roman neighbors, they actively undermined these practices.

The early Christians' resistance to infant exposure was not some eccentric quirk, nor something to be glossed over quickly. The practice arguably helped launch Christianity. Rodney Stark, Distinguished Professor of the Social Sciences at Baylor University, has argued that Christian attitudes and practices towards the sick and vulnerable drove conversion rates to Christianity.[4] Put roughly: people joined up with the Christians often not because of a convincing piece of theology (let alone an entire book like this one!), but rather because of the Christian practice of caring for those that others would not. The early Christian leader Tertullian arrived at the same diagnosis: "It is mainly the deeds of a love so noble that lead many to put a brand upon us. See how they love one another, they say."[5]

So, early Christians followed a different path than their contemporaries, and this path wound up being deeply attractive to others. But what set them down the path to begin with? What moved them to care for vulnerable members of society when the surrounding culture told them not to bother? The answer is found in a core Christian idea that is both familiar and radical: early Christians held an unwavering conviction in the fundamental dignity and equality of every human being. We could call this idea the basic equality view. The basic equality view, in its initial articulation, was based on Christ's commandment to love each other (Jn 15: 12-13), and his life lived in service to the outcast and vulnerable. If each human life exhibits inherent dignity, and if each human life is worth as much as any other, then infant exposure must be called out for what it is: an attack on the most vulnerable among us.

I take it that all of us (Christians and non-Christians alike) agree with the assessment of the early Christians. Infant exposure ought not be practiced because it is a violation of vulnerable human life. In the twenty-first century, however, we can take this conclusion for granted. We have grown familiar with language about dignity and equality, and with the underlying basic equality view—it is enshrined in our talk of human rights, in the Declaration of Independence ("all men are created equal"), and in our everyday interactions with each other. The basic equality view seems so familiar as to be morally blasé. As ethicist and theologian Charles Camosy notes:

> Many of us rightly believe that human equality is one of those foundational ideas necessary for a culture to be minimally decent in the first place. Most of the Western world operates as if it is just obvious that all human beings are equal. Indeed, this may be the great moral insight of our culture, held by the overwhelming majority of us across a diverse range of political affiliations and tribes.[6]

That's a good thing. Yet we ought not take it for granted, nor ignore the basic equality view's lineage. The outlook owes its heritage not to any philosophical school or secular tradition, but rather to the beliefs and practices of early Christians. Indeed, as Camosy discusses, "even secular giants like Jürgen Habermas have come to appreciate the unique role Christian thought has played in what he calls 'egalitarian universalism.' There is no alternative to Christianity, says Habermas, upon which to ground our contemporary notion of universal human rights."[7]

# Dignity, Equality, Credentials

To understand the basic equality view better—and to make this familiar idea just a bit unfamiliar—it will be helpful to contrast it with a very different way of thinking about the foundation of human value. Consider, then, that many philosophical schools, social traditions, and individual beliefs grow from the idea that human value does *not* come simply from being human, but rather from certain characteristics humans possess (or don't). Let's call outlooks like these credential views, since they claim human value is conferred by possessing some credential or set of credentials. Credential views thus operate like overworked TSA officers—rather than distributing value willy-nilly, they check for credentials before signing approval.

Some of the most morally atrocious outlooks are credential views: racism divvies up human worth along racial lines; sexism along the lines of human biology; the list goes on. In chapter 2, I also introduced the idea of ableism, an outlook that would have us dole out human value based on what individual humans can or cannot do. All these moral outlooks are credential views, since each claims humans are valuable not simply because they are human, but rather because they possess some supposedly valuable characteristic. Wherever they turn up, credential views locate value by looking past our shared humanity and instead to some other credential—for example, membership in a certain race or the possession of certain abilities. The problem: whatever credential gets picked out by a credential view, it is inevitably a characteristic that not all of us share.

When considered in extreme forms like racism and ableism, you likely reject credential views outright. At least, I hope you do. Racism, sexism, ableism: these patterns of thinking have consistently led to moral atrocities, broken relationships, toxic social practices, and the consolidation of control in the hands of the powerful. But there are subtler credential views. Consider, for example, philosophical views that latch onto some seemingly dignified feature to explain what makes humans distinctive. The seventeenth-century philosopher René Descartes claimed cognition makes humans what we are: humans are capable of thinking, doubting, pondering, philosophizing. Other creatures are not. The eighteenth-century philosopher Immanuel Kant, by contrast, moved rationality to center stage. Humans are rational. Dogs and mosquitos are not. And for the contemporary philosopher Peter Singer, what makes a human unique is being a "rational and self-conscious being that is aware of itself as a distinct entity with a past and a future."[8] Humans take vacations and craft wish lists. Other animals—smart though they may be—do neither.

On their face, these observations may seem on track. Yet if we attach *value* to the characteristics the philosophers identify as making humans distinctive, all these ideas have potential to morph into a credential view. Frontload Kantian rationality as foundational to human value, and some neurodivergent people may not make the cut. People with schizophrenia or obsessive-compulsive disorder, after all, don't always behave in recognizably rational ways. Emphasize instead our ability to think? Young children and Alzheimer's patients fall short. What about Singer's idea, the idea that laying plans makes us distinctive? If we hang our hats here, then scores of people—infants, cognitively disabled adults, those at the end of their lives—fall off our moral radars. In fact, Singer has recognized this as an implication of his view: in certain contexts he defends the killing of children.[9] Not *quite* infant exposure, but something close to it. Here's the lesson: if we attempt to ground human value in something other than the basic equality view, we risk coming full circle, back to something chillingly like the ancient Roman view. Generally, any philosophical outlook that attempts to locate human distinctiveness *in some characteristic* inevitably divides humanity up into haves and have-nots.

## Credentials beyond the Ivory Tower

It isn't just philosophers who endorse the credential view. This view lurks often just below the surface of our social and individual lives. In fact, once you know what to look for, credential views are tough to miss. MTV Cribs gives tours of the homes of the rich and famous, not the bungalows of lower middle-class families. Glossy magazines celebrate certain bodies and gloss over others. Top athletes are showered with endorsements while disabled veterans jockey for entry-level jobs. As a professor, I often see my students attach their personal worth to their GPA, as if a 4.0 student mattered more than a student struggling to maintain a 2.5. Not all these practices add up to explicit endorsement of the credential view. Yet all of them strike a clear note: people should be valued not simply because of their shared humanity, but instead because of what they can do, how they look, what they own, or their status in society. Let's consider more carefully other ways the credential view turns up beyond the ivory tower.

### COVID-19, Ventilators, and QALY Scores

I'm writing this book in 2022, having slogged through the COVID-19 pandemic for over two years. During this period, the world has begun speaking the language of professional bioethicists and epidemiologists, as we worked to keep ourselves and others healthy, and to traverse our lives together. Early in the pandemic, for example, the nightly news often featured discussions about how to distribute ventilators. Those who became very sick from COVID needed artificial ventilation to assist with breathing. Indeed, *not* being put on a ventilator could mean death. The problem: we didn't always have enough ventilators to go around. So we had to decide: who gets a ventilator first?

In many of these conversations, credential views lingered just beneath the surface. Ventilators, pundits claimed, should be reserved for those people *who matter most*. In other words: the young or the healthy or the socially useful. The implication: not the very old or the chronically ill or the unemployed or those on the margins of society. Don't have the right credentials? You're not seeing a ventilator any time soon.

Now, the problem here does not lie in resource distribution itself. When it comes to divvying up scarce resources, *someone* needs to get them. We can't hem and haw while needy patients struggle to breathe. So we can't be blamed for deciding that one person gets a ventilator while another does not. And prioritizing some feature—some credential—is inevitable in a fair distribution. Yet we must tread carefully when our decision-procedure focuses on credentials other than medical need. Provide ventilators to those who *need* them most? That could lead us to an ethically appropriate distribution. But all too often, other credentials creep in. Don't focus so much on need, we tell ourselves. Focus instead on youth. Or health. Or wealth. Or social status. But what if you need a ventilator and don't have those credentials? Well, good luck on your own.

This way of thinking about resource distribution did not arrive on the scene with COVID. It has played a role in decision-making contexts for a long time. Consider the Quality Adjusted Life Year (QALY), a unit of measurement that has long been used by economists, bioethics, and doctors in decision-making. A QALY score aims to capture the length and quality of someone's life with a numerical value. A healthy teen from the charming suburbs would thus likely be assigned a high QALY score, since they have many years in front of them, and presumably, a high quality of life (who doesn't like a charming suburb?). By contrast, a disabled senior in an assisted living facility would likely be assigned a low QALY score (because, the assumption goes, aren't assisted living facilities kind of depressing?).

QALY scores have proved especially useful—and especially nefarious—because we can use them to calculate concrete values for making medical decisions. Should we follow Plan A? What about Plan B? Plan C? Once you have calculated QALY scores, the decision becomes easy. Simply pick the plan that produces the highest QALY score. Don't go thinking, moreover, that QALY scores are mere fodder for theoreticians. The National Institute for Health and Clinical Excellence in the United Kingdom is required to use "cost per QALY" in making its decisions.[10]

What's the problem with QALY scores? Superficially, these scores seem to provide an objective strategy for doling out resources. What can get more objective than math?! Scratch the surface, however, and you see that we have been hoodwinked. QALY scores may *seem* objective, but they are anything but. The problem lies in the idea that we can assign a numerical value to someone's quality of life, and in the features that are typically highlighted as conferring a high value. What contributes to a high quality of life score? Wealth; youth; health; privilege. Sound familiar? QALY scores, while seemingly objective, inevitably give high marks to privileged teens from charming suburbs, not disabled seniors from vulnerable populations. The numbers distract us from what is really going on. Not an objective decision-making procedure, but instead, a formalized credential view.

## Trolley Problems and Autonomous Vehicles

If you have a minute, visit the website for the Massachusetts Institute of Technology's Moral Machine (https://www.moral-machine.net). The "machine" presents a lo-fi illustration of a car barreling towards two groups of pedestrians and asks us to make gut-wrenching decisions. The car must hit one group or the other, killing the lot. Which one? In one scenario: choose between hitting three senior citizens on your right, or two children and a dog on your left. In another: a health care worker on your left, or a barricade that will kill the driver on the right. In yet another: three bank robbers on the left, or one pregnant woman on the right.

The Moral Machine is no mere exercise in fatalist thinking. It is instead motivated by a real moral quandary all of us will face soon: how to navigate the implementation of autonomous vehicles? Autonomous vehicles are cars that are driven automatically. Think of the Google car, or a next generation Tesla, piloted by Siri instead of Sara. We have good reason to think that in the future autonomous vehicles will be widespread. We also have good reason to think that they will be safer than manually driven cars. An on-board algorithm, after all, won't fall asleep at the wheel or get distracted by a text message or miss an exit while belting out "Don't Stop Believin.'" Yet as we make the move to autonomous vehicles, we will have to make tough decisions about how the vehicles should operate. Should they save their "drivers" at all costs? Or should they avoid certain kinds of accidents (e.g., those involving children) over others? Or should they simply maximize the number of lives saved? As we implement autonomous vehicles, these are the kinds of questions we will have to answer. And the Moral Machine—which has collected more than forty million decisions—is working to provide data to inform our decisions.

The Moral Machine, however, is also deeply indebted to the patterns of thinking that are hallmarks of a credential view. In fact, the very set up of the Moral Machine *assumes* a credential view. In asking us to weigh the relative value of someone's occupation, age, and criminal status, it assumes that these features are morally relevant. That as we make our decision about how an autonomous vehicle should operate, *of course* we'll want to know how old the bystanders are, whether they work in a useful occupation, and whether they have broken any laws. The Moral Machine doesn't even get off the ground without taking on board a credential view.

Despite these problematic origins, the Moral Machine has nevertheless gathered gobs of useful information about how real people deploy the credential view. For example, people across the globe tend to show a strong preference for sparing the young over the old. And for sparing those with high status over low status, those who are fit over those who are not, and females over males. Participants are much more likely to spare a pregnant woman than a homeless man, more likely to spare a homeless man than an old man, and more likely to spare a dog than a criminal. That last result especially should give us pause, given how it may play out in the context of criminal justice.

The results get even more interesting—if that's the right word for it—when broken down by region and culture. For example, those from Eastern areas (Asia and certain parts of the Middle East) show less bias towards youth—being a senior in Eastern areas is not as disadvantageous as it is in other regions. Those from Latin and Central America, by contrast, are particularly likely to spare women and physically fit people. Individualistic cultures (those cultures that emphasize the importance of individuals over groups) are more likely to look to overall numbers in making their decisions. Strangely, cultures with less economic inequality show *more* inequality in their preference of rich over poor. [11]

The Moral Machine, although built on faulty foundations, thus serves a useful purpose: it maps the precise contours of credential views, and how these views have taken root in various parts of the world. The Moral Machine identifies ways in which humans have elevated certain credentials over others, and how our geographic and cultural location has influenced our rankings. This is undeniably a great service, as it shows us what is going on under the hood of our decision-making and ethical thinking. It also teaches a clear lesson: the credential view is no mere academic theory. It is instead foundational to our everyday decision-making.

## Burnout

A quick internet search of the word "burnout" turns up scores of recent articles. Here's a sample:

- "Health-care workers call for government help as burnout worsens and staff shortages increase" ~*Yahoo News Canada*
- "How to find a new job when you're burned out" ~*Vox*
- "Stressed and burned out? Quitting your job may not help" ~*CNBC*
- "Why Gen Z workers are already so burned out" ~*BBC*
- "Addressing employee burnout: Are you solving the right problem?" ~*McKinsey*

I could go on. And on. And then on some more.

Don't go thinking, though, that "burnout" is some made-up, journalistic buzzword. It isn't. While burnout isn't a formal medical diagnosis, the Mayo Clinic features an entry on it, describing it as "a special type of work-related stress—a state of physical or emotional exhaustion that also involves a sense of reduced accomplishment and loss of personal identity."[12] Lost your concentration at work or school? Cynical about your job? Scroll social media when you're bumped up against a tight deadline? Find it difficult to feel good about your accomplishments? You may be experiencing burnout. Once you have learned to identify burnout, you will notice it cropping up in the lives of many those around you. Maybe even in your own.

What causes burnout? That's a complicated question to answer. The Mayo Clinic proffers several explanations: a lack of control over one's professional life, unclear job expectations, dysfunctional workplace dynamics, extremes of activity, lack of social support, and work-life imbalance. Now, I'm not one to quibble with the Mayo Clinic, but I would like to offer a different—or perhaps simply *deeper*—diagnosis. Credential views. Sure, burnout may stem from a feeling of not being in control of your life, or from an off-kilter work-life balance. But what are the root causes of *these*? Why do we find ourselves obsessed with school, or with our jobs? And why do so many of us feel a kind of quiet desperation—a complete lack of control—every time we clock in for another shift or late-night study session?

At least in part because we're told time and time again that our value comes not from who we are as humans, but rather from some credential we must earn: from our contributions, from how we perform, from our job title, or from the grades we receive. We are told this in subtle ways and not-so-subtle ways by our bosses, friends, families, and culture. It gets whispered to us when aunties ask whether we made Honor Roll. It lingers in the background when we break the ice at cocktail hour by talking about our careers. And it is the message which bombards us when ads and reality TV and celebrities shout that we have "made it" if only we can afford a little nicer car, a little better house, a little more stylish pair of jeans.

Now, not all these practices amount to explicit endorsement of the credential view. Some of the practices may even be good—we need *something* to talk about with strangers at cocktail hour, and aiming for the Honor Roll is all-in-all a good thing. Yet each of these practices—and scores of others—carry an underlying message: people should be valued not simply because of their shared humanity, but instead because of what they can do, how they look, how they perform, or their status in society. Take that message on board, and you start thinking about yourself less and less as a human with fundamental dignity, and more and more as a cog in a machine. No wonder burnout runs rampant. The credential view is no stuffy academic theory. It instead provides the unacknowledged background hum to much of our twenty-first century lives.

## Basic Equality Redux

Once we have learned to identify the credential view—and once we have seen how pervasive it is—the basic equality view stands out for what it is, and for its countercultural flavor. The credential view tells us that our age or ability or social contributions or job titles give us worth and meaning. That some credential we earn (or is given to us by genetic or social lottery) makes our lives worth living. And that people with credentials matter more than people without them. That the rich, the powerful, the young, and the privileged matter more than the poor, the vulnerable, the disadvantaged, the unprivileged. In stark contrast to the credential view, the basic equality view works as:

a bulwark against the kinds of utilitarian approaches which would target the most vulnerable among us and discard them in the name of producing better consequences for others. Genuine human equality means that accidental traits like age, level of ability, reliance on others, level of self-awareness, rationality or autonomy do not affect the value of a human being—which comes from their nature as human beings and nothing else.[13]

Need a remedy to those views that would place people with certain abilities or looks on a pedestal? Look no further than the basic equality view. This radical view attracted early converts to Christianity. And the idea continues to be attractive today. Yet at the same time it is a radical view that stands athwart many of the practices and assumptions we bring to our everyday lives.

Consider, though, an objection to the basic equality view. Does this not collapse into an "everyone gets a trophy" mentality? If so, that's a problem. No one likes the saccharine idea that we all deserve a gold medal, just for showing up. That really, at the end of the day, LeBron James and Magnus Carlsen and Katie Ledecky and [INSERT YOUR HEROES HERE] don't *deserve* their trophies or NBA contracts or Olympic medals. That everyone is a winner. If we embrace the basic equality view, do we have to embrace *that*? If so, no thanks.

The objection is important. But it also misses the mark. Here's why: the basic equality view insists everyone *starts* at the same place. That each of us matters simply because we are human, regardless of what we do, or what we accomplish, or what society deems most important. The everyone gets a trophy mindset, by contrast, says everyone *finishes* at the same place. That each of us deserves a spot on the winner's pedestal. That we should ignore the differences in our levels of ability, and the degree of excellence some of us can achieve. That's an obviously misguided approach, one that grows from an intentionally skewed view of the world.

The objection, however, highlights something the credential view does get right. In almost every way you care to consider, humans are *not* equal. We differ in our IQs and our ability to swim a butterfly and our capacity to play chess. We vary in height and hand-eye coordination. We're wildly unequal in our creativity and knack for schmoozing at wedding receptions. Not all of us can engage in abstract reasoning. And only some of us can determine which wine would pair well with the evening's entrée. These differences are not a bad thing. In fact, they are a good thing. I'll never be Katie Ledecky or Magnus Carlsen or LeBron James or, for that matter, my wife or cousin or friend down the street. In different ways, all far outpace me in their abilities. And we should celebrate these differences, not gloss over them.

The problem with the credential view, then, does not lie in recognizing human difference or in celebrating human accomplishment. The problem rather comes with attaching our worth as humans to these differences. It is one thing to admit that LeBron James is better than I am at basketball. It is something very different to say that his worth as a human comes from this ability. The first observation is obvious. The second carries with it a nefarious lie: that some of us matter more than others.

We should, therefore, celebrate the fact that LeBron James excels at basketball, and that only one Olympic athlete finishes with the gold. And yes, that only one Little League team wins the tournament. Humans differ in our level of ability, and we can and should celebrate the accomplishments of those who rise to a level above the rest of us. The basic equality view need not lead us to abandon this practice, nor need it collapse into the idea that everyone gets a trophy. The basic equality view rather insists that despite our differences, there is one way in which we are equal—in our fundamental worth and value as human beings.

All this should provide a sense of the basic equality view on an intellectual level. But what does the basic equality view look like when incorporated into a life? We have already seen the answer. The lives of Mother Teresa, Damien of Molokai, and scores of saints like them like them look as they do because they are built on the basic equality view. The idea of fundamental human dignity led Saint Damien to live among those with leprosy. And it steered Saint Mother Teresa to share her life with the poorest of the poor. Once you see these figures as embracing every human as infinitely valuable—and rejecting the credential view entirely—their lives start to click. They become just a touch less incomprehensible. On an intellectual level, the basic equality view is already countercultural. But when lived out consistently, the basic equality view morphs boring lives into extraordinary ones. It turns ordinary sinners into saints.

There is, however, more to the story. The fallen dignity view—the outlook lived out by the saints—builds on the foundation of the basic equality view. That's true. But it also takes on board a second, seemingly very different idea: the idea that humans are fallen. That we are sinful. That despite our infinite worth and fundamental value, we fail to attain perfection. Time and time again. That we are *fallen*. Without this piece, we'll never understand the lives of the saints. Nor will we have the resources to mount a response to new technologies of human enhancement. Eventually, we'll start working on that response. But first, let's turn to consider the idea of human fallenness on its own terms. As we'll see, this idea is just as countercultural as the basic equality view, though for very different reasons.

## Human Fallenness

Shortly after his election, Pope Francis—formerly Cardinal Jorge Mario Bergoglio—was asked: "Who is Jorge Mario Bergoglio?" The Pope's answer? "I am a sinner. This is the most accurate definition. It is not a figure of speech, or a literary genre. I am a sinner."[14] This answer flouts interview conventions. Nothing in his response about being a "born leader" or "a humble servant of the people" or even about being a "just a poor kid from the neighborhood." None of that. Instead: "a sinner." Not the answer many would expect from a world leader.

The answer, however, should not shock someone shaped by a Christian outlook. While Christians have long endorsed the basic equality view, they have balanced this optimistic thesis with the realist's idea of human fallenness. According to Christians—early and contemporary alike—we humans "have sinned and fall short of the glory of God" (Rom 3:23). We "like sheep have gone astray; we have all turned to our own way" (Is 53:6). We have set ourselves "against God's love for us and [turned] our hearts away from it."[15] We have followed in the steps of Adam and Eve, rejecting the plan that God has laid out. We have, in a word, fallen.

Christianity, in fact, makes little sense without the thesis of fallenness. At the heart of Christianity rests the claim that Christ saves us from our sin. But who needs saving if we are already perfect? Who needs to be lifted by Christ if we have not fallen? Reject the idea of human fallenness, and you eliminate your need for a savior. Sans fallenness, the Christian outlook crumbles.

Of course, the devil is in the details (quite literally, in this case). *Precisely* what it means for humans to be fallen has confounded theologians for centuries. Calvinists claim that we are "totally depraved," that every aspect of human life has been marred by the fall. According to Calvin: "the will is so utterly . . . corrupted in every part as to produce nothing but evil."[16] Talk about fallenness. Catholics, by contrast, approach the topic differently, arguing that human dignity shines through our fallenness more brightly. According to Catholics, we can, with God's help, be "righteous" like Noah (Gn 6:9), finding "favor in the sight of the LORD" (Gn 6: 8). Fallen? Yes. But not totally depraved.

For now, though, skip the theology lecture. Debates about how to understand fallenness have already filled shelves of bookcases. You don't want to read all that. Just this one book will do. Let's focus, then, on where we can agree. Christians—Calvinists and Catholics alike—may disagree about the details, but all can pray the Jesus Prayer with a clean conscience: "Lord Jesus, son of the Living God, have mercy on me, a sinner." Christians across the board reject the idea that humans are good "as is" or that we can achieve perfection on our own. And they can recognize that Pope Francis's comment cuts to the heart of the faith, and of Christian self-understanding.

The idea that humans are fallen stands central to Christianity. But we needn't peruse the library's theology section or even subscribe to Christianity to arrive at the idea. A survey of the last hundred years confirms it. The terror of the Third Reich; the atrocities of the Khmer Rouge; the Dresden fire-bombing: making a list of world events to confirm human fallenness is unfortunately easy.

We can also confirm human fallenness by bringing things closer to home. Truth be told, an honest moment's self-reflection will usually do the trick. All too often, we act with alternative motives, fail to give others the benefit of the doubt, elevate self-serving interests rather than those of others, and act in ways that primarily serve to puff up our own egos. In our better moments, and with God's grace, we may overcome these impulses. Yet they linger in the background, and without vigilance we slip back into them: in our social media posts; in conversations with family members; in the rat race at work. As the Protestant theologian Reinhold Niebuhr once observed: "I still think the 'London Times Literary Supplement' was substantially correct when it wrote some years ago: 'The doctrine of original sin is the only empirically verifiable doctrine of the Christian faith.'"[17] Reject the idea that humans are fallen? A quick review of last week will likely change your mind.

## Human Fallenness as Countercultural

Obvious as the idea of human fallenness may be, it strikes a deeply countercultural note. We have already seen that the basic equality view stands opposed to many cultural practices and implicit beliefs. The same goes for human fallenness. The idea may be obvious in one sense, but also resists contemporary culture. In what follows, we'll begin to see the scope of this resistance.

## Life Hacking

Joseph M. Reagle, Jr., Associate Professor of Communication Studies at Northeastern University, wrote the book on life hacking. Well, the *scholarly* book on life hacking. According to Reagle, life hacking "sits at the intersection of technology, culture, and larger concerns about work, health, relationship, and meaning. It is the manifestation of the hacker ethos, an individualistic and rational approach of systemization and experimentation."[18] A good life hack improves "life via a systematic approach" by offering "a novel solution or fix, which is often shared."[19] Life hackers aim to eliminate chores, speed up tasks, and short-circuit everyday problems.

Now, I like life hacking as much as the next guy. Okay, probably a little more than the next guy. As a parent to three small children, homeowner of a moody 1960s split-level, and overworked professor sprinting towards my fortieth birthday, I need to lean on every trick in the book. A craft that can keep my kids entertained using a box of leftover pasta and a set of markers? A method to fold t-shirts in under three seconds? A new stretch that will take the edge off my lower back pain? Sign me up. And keep the hacks coming.

There's nothing wrong with life hacking. A good life hack can free up time and leave us feeling satisfied at having beat the system. On the surface, life hacks promise simple ways to make life just a little better (or easier, or healthier). Incorporate extra fiber in your life! Adopt a fail-proof method for keeping your kitchen clean! Level-up your ab workout in just five minutes a day! All good things? Sure. Who doesn't appreciate a clean home and six-pack abs?

Go beyond the superficial promises of life hacking, however, and the practice starts to look more questionable. For one thing, the life hacker's view of the world can often *over*simplify the world. For the life hacker, Reagle observes, "most everything is conceived as a system: it is modular, composed of parts, which can be decomposed and recomposed."[20] For the life hacker (and for you and me, in life hacking mode), folding a pile of laundry and whipping up a batch of breakfast tacos are not merely everyday hassles or tasks. They should instead be understood as series of steps, steps that can be analyzed for efficiency and then ramped up, eliminated, or swapped out as needed. This way of thinking may very well help us create a more efficient life. Yet it is overly simplistic to think about our every tasks as "governed by algorithmic rules, which can be understood, optimized, and subverted."[21] My laundry routine, for example, is not *just* a set of steps to me: it contains echoes of my personal history (I fold t-shirts how my mom taught me), cultural overtones (I forego ironing in ways that would raise eyebrows in certain social circles), and personal preferences (I sometimes linger over laundry to decompress from my day). Life hacking reduces our daily lives to sets of optimal and suboptimal steps, all pointed towards to the goal of arriving efficiently at a single outcome: folded laundry or weight loss or entertainment for the kids. In reality our lives are far richer than that.

More problematically, however, the life hacker's outlook ignores an elephant in the room—the fact that humans are hard-wired to be inefficient, easily distracted, and prone to give up too soon. The fact that we often act with problematic motives; that we rarely succeed at ridding ourselves of biases and prejudices; that we often serve ourselves first instead of the most vulnerable among us. The fact that we are, in a word, fallen. For the Christian, we have seen, the idea of human fallenness is both obvious on reflection and crucial for understanding ourselves. For the life hacker, by contrast, human fallenness is a glitch in the system, a bug to be analyzed and overcome. Here's Reagle on the outlook:

> How do we manage our counterproductive fear, anger, sloth, addictions, and other unwanted behaviors? Just as we manage our dysfunctional scratching of poison ivy by trimming our nails and wearing mittens to bed, we need similar 'tricks' for the rest of life.[22]

The promises of the life hacker may be superficially helpful, but often carry a chorus of whispers: *life needn't feel so hard; your flaws can be eliminated; a perfect life is just one technique away.* The popularity of life hacking thus highlights just how countercultural the idea of fallenness is.

Ironically, however, life hacking does not merely gloss over human fallenness. In its excessive forms, life hacking also *illustrates* human fallenness. As Reagle observes, life hacking often morphs from a culture of helpful tips into morally problematic practices. Some hackers—so-called pickup artists—use hacking techniques to rack up sexual exploits, taking advantage of human psychology to boost their own egos.[23] Other hackers game systems in ways that are clearly unfair, stretching tax loopholes and coupon cutting to unsustainable extremes. Still other hacking practices ooze with the kind of privilege that is available only to the elite few. For example, minimalism—the practice of hacking through excess by trimming one's possessions—may look virtuous on the surface, but on reflection, is available only to people with an extensive economic safety net. Reagle similarly points to the lives of Ben Franklin and Tim Ferriss, life hackers *par excellence*. Both writers, Reagle admits, provide plenty of helpful tips. Yet *Poor Richard's Almanack* and *The Four-Hour Workweek* often ignore ways in which these tips provide convenience for an elite few by offloading drudgery to others:

> Franklin was prolific, but he gave little thought to how his wife, Deborah Read, made it possible for him to live such a prolific life. He was also able to delegate much drudgery to his enslaved personal servants— before becoming an abolitionist later in life. In turn, Ferriss has accomplished a lot in his four-hour work-weeks only by outsourcing his tedious tasks to [low-paid workers in countries such as the Philippines and India].[24]

Life hacking can shave off work time, but in doing so, perpetuate unjust systems. The very kinds of injustice that are hallmarks of human fallenness. In its very attempt to ignore human fallenness, life hacking ends up providing an excellent example of it.

## Self-Help

We have been discussing life hacking as if it were a new idea. It isn't. Rather, life hacking joins a genre usually labeled "self-help," a style of thinking so central to contemporary life that it has earned its own aisle in near every bookstore. If you can stomach it, browse that aisle sometime. Most titles provide an honest summary of their contents. *The 7 Habits of Highly Effective People*; *How to Win Friends and Influence People*; *The Power of Positive Thinking*: all aim to deliver exactly what their titles promise. *The Secret* is a bit more provocative. The secret? What could it be? I'll save you fifteen dollars: the secret is to visualize what you want every day until you get it.

Recently, self-help has navigated from the bookstore to the internet. Lifestyle YouTubers sharing tips for a better life; social media influencers guiding followers on their journeys; meditation apps promising a calmer life: all could be filed under the heading of self-help. Fad diets; daytime TV; CrossFit; home improvement shows; Peloton: most probably make the cut as well. There's no need, however, for us to police the boundaries of *precisely* what counts as self-help. Whether we are scrolling Instagram, streaming podcasts, or rifling through the bookshelves at Aunt Maisie's house, we likely confront and consume a fair bit of the genre. As Reagle observes, "strains of self-help culture ... have been embedded in the national DNA since *Poor Richard's Almanack*."[25]

That's not necessarily a bad thing. Like life hacking, self-help can offer useful tips and tricks. Sometimes, it offers wisdom. Consider some of Dale Carnegie's advice in *How to Win Friends and Influence People*: smile; give honest and sincere appreciation; become genuinely interested in other people; make the other person feel important; if you are wrong, admit it quickly and emphatically; talk about your own mistakes before criticizing the other person.[26] All good advice? Sure. At least most of the time. Some of Carnegie's tips may even be good moral advice, advice that if followed will help you become a better person. The same can be said for much of the self-help genre. Follow your average lifestyle YouTuber's advice, and your life may get a bit better. Perhaps *you* will even become a bit better. There is a reason why Carnegie's book has remained a sensation nearly a hundred years after its publication.

Like life hacking, however, the shiny veneer of self-help only runs so deep. For starters, the one-size-fits-all approach of the genre often encourages us to ignore our differences, the very differences that provide life with its flavor. Not all of us greet every morning with a smile, and that's not a bad thing. Indeed, I am friends with some people not despite but because of their biting sarcasm. And there's a reason that satires of lifestyle YouTube are nearly as popular as the real thing—we enjoy seeing a more honest approach. Depending on our cultural context, moreover, some of the practices advocated by self-helpers might do more harm than good. A beaming smile, slap on the back, and booming hello might inspire confidence in a Manhattan boardroom, but distaste among Japanese company men. Likewise, I run in circles (most very nerdy ones) where a well-polished persona is more likely to raise eyebrows than foster friendships. Self-help, like life hacking, may provide helpful tips, but rests on an overly simplified outlook.

And the problems run deeper still. One problem goes to the heart of our discussion: self-help, like life hacking, all too often ignores the fact that humans are fallen. That we are imperfect. That we sometimes act for self-serving ends. That we often see what needs to be done, and then do precisely the opposite. That we are, in Pope Francis's words, *sinners*. *The Secret* promises that if we visualize our desires, we'll get them. It doesn't pause to reflect on the fact that some of our desires are bad for ourselves, others, or both. Maybe I really want a new Corvette or a more prestigious job. Have I paused to think about whether either will do me any good? Or have I stopped to reflect on the fact that visualizing a new Corvette every day may well make me more materialistic? Or that a well-run charity might be a better use of my resources? Self-help, by definition, encourages us to *help ourselves*. That can be a good thing, but only if paired with honest moral reflection about who we are, and why we need help.

Self-help, like life hacking, also illustrates a deep irony: ignore human fallenness and you may very well slip into it. I'll admit it: I have been listening to the audio version of *How to Win Friends and Influence People*. My reaction? There's a lot of good advice here. But also: *I hope evil people aren't listening*. Consider again some of its advice: smile; become genuinely interested in other people; make the other person feel important. When you read this advice generously, it seems decent (if a bit obvious). If you read it cynically, however, the advice starts to sound like the playbook of a cult leader. Or a conman. Or a malevolent dictator. The advice proffered by self-help may indeed be effective, but rises to the level of being good only when paired with morally upright intentions. Paired with the kinds of intentions that characterize fallen humans, self-help builds up the worst kind of behavior.

Nearly three hundred years ago, the philosopher Immanuel Kant anticipated this. "The only thing that is good without qualification," Kant argued, "is a good will."[27] In other words: the best tips and tricks won't do any good unless paired with intentions that are *already* good. Pair self-help with fallen intentions, and you get fallen results. This observation led Kant to criticize self-help under the heading of "popular practical philosophy":

What it turns out is a disgusting hotch-potch of sec-
ond-hand observations and semi-rational principles
on which the empty-headed regale themselves,
because this is something that can be used in the
chit-chat of daily life. . . . What we shall encounter
in an amazing medley is at one time the particular
character of human nature, another perfection, at
another happiness; here moral feeling and there the
fear of God; something of this and something of that.[28]

And you thought I was being hard on the genre.

But don't miss the important point: the point is not to
convince you to give up lifestyle YouTube or cancel your
subscription to Peloton or return your copy of *The Secret*. The
point I want to make is subtler than this: that self-help can
have its place, but that when it ignores human fallenness—as
it does all too often—the genre can quickly sour from good
advice to malevolent guidebook. Generally, the popularity of
self-help illustrates the degree to which we ignore human
fallenness, concentrating on quick fixes without going to
the core of the problem.

### Social Media

Here's a challenge: spend some time today scrolling through
old social media posts, and flag those that highlight *your
fallenness*. How often do you use social media to expose your
frailty? Admit you got something wrong? Capture moments
when you acted with bad intentions or said something spite-
ful or took an imbalanced approached to life? If you're like
me, you will be hard pressed to find much. Most of us use
social media to paint a photoshopped picture of ourselves.
We remove our wrinkles, ignore our failings, and overemphasize the glitzy side of our lives. The resulting picture is
not false—not exactly—but is misleading.

There has been plenty of discussion about the psychological harm caused by our collective habits on social media. Professors, pundits, and parents have argued that the unrealistic pictures we paint on social media can ramp up depression and tank self-esteem. I don't doubt it. Here, though, I want to focus on a different point—the way our lives on social media resist the idea of human fallenness. According to this idea, we have seen, humans are imperfect, made whole only through the grace of God. We are, in Pope Francis's words, *sinners*. Our lives as seen through social media, however, would lead us to a very different conclusion. The average Instagram feed tells a story about a life that is sweet not sinful, fabulous not fallen.

An objection: what about social media posts and accounts that aim to "get real"? You know what I mean. Selfies sans makeup. Kids melting down in the background. Botched cookies. Failed craft projects. Don't these posts highlight human fallenness rather than hide it under the rug?

An honest answer: kind of. These posts are certainly more honest the touched-up photos that dominate social media. They may even balance out some of the psychological harm created by glossy Instagram feeds. It feels good to know that not everyone's life looks like it was torn from the latest issue of *Teen Vogue* or *Magnolia Home* or *Condé Nast Traveler*. Yet posts that aim to "get real" typically present a façade of imperfection more than imperfection itself. Indeed, getting real is itself a meme, one that can be done well or poorly, and one that rarely reveals actual problems. Post pictures of overcooked brownies? That's okay. But don't go posting about how your ego tanked a friendship, or how you failed to give your child the benefit of the doubt, or the everyday bad habits you've failed to kick. This would be too much. And besides, it would make for a boring feed. Best stick to selfies before you've combed your hair.

Here's the point I'm making: social media *itself* often functions as a filter, one that glosses over the fallenness that characterizes humanity. Like life hacking and self-help, we turn to Instagram and Twitter and Facebook to excise those parts of our lives we'd prefer remain hidden. And in doing so, we participate in a cultural practice that runs counter to the Christian (and, on reflection, obvious) thesis that humans are imperfect.

Things needn't be this way. Contrast the average social media user with a story told about the Christian theologian G.K. Chesterton. Prompted by a newspaper column with the question "What is wrong with the world?" Chesterton submitted a two-word reply: "I am." Chesterton's response, while apocryphal, captures the Christian outlook. It leans into rather than shies away from the thesis of human fallenness. It also provides a counterpoint to the approach many of us take to social media. Few social media feeds suggest that the problem with the world is *me*.

Like life hacking and self-help, however, our lives on social media can ignore but not eliminate human fallenness. To see the evidence, you need only scroll through comments of a controversial Twitter post or YouTube video. Forget bridges. Comboxes are where the trolls live now. And what they say could be used as a highlights reel of what is wrong with the world.

There are also other ways human fallenness shines through social media, despite our best efforts. Take just one example: Chatbot Tay. Launched by Microsoft in 2016, Chatbot Tay was a Twitter account powered by artificial intelligence and designed to mimic the tweets of an American teen. Things went south quickly. Twitter users bombarded Tay with offensive, R-rated messages. Tay's algorithm picked up on the themes, and quickly followed suit. Within sixteen hours, Tay had become a vulgar, feminist-hating, Nazi-loving, racist troll. I won't repeat her tweets. Google them at your own risk. Microsoft quickly moved Tay offline. A failed attempt at public relations. But an excellent example at revealing the fallenness that festers in the servers of Silicon Valley.

## Beware the Schopenhauer Sulk

Humans are fallen. Imperfect in our altruism, we serve ourselves before others and allow our thoughts and actions to be nudged this way and that by bad habits, biases, stereotypes, and phobias. A quick glance at the headlines—not to mention our own diaries—makes the point obvious. Yet as we have seen, many of our cultural practices resist the idea. From life hacking to self-help to social media, we often act as if all is okay *with us*, that the problems of the world lie elsewhere. Human fallenness may be evident in the abstract and in our honest moments of self-reflection. In our public lives, however, the idea begets controversy.

Yet we must take care. Overemphasize human fallenness, and you slip into cynicism. Dwell too much on the headlines or on our individual foibles, and we can slide into a view of ourselves as irredeemable or beyond saving or rotten to the core. Arthur Schopenhauer, a nineteenth-century philosopher, embraced this pessimistic outlook:

> That thousands had lived in happiness and joy would never do away with the anguish and death-agony of one individual; and just as little does my present well-being undo my previous sufferings. Therefore, were the evil in the world even a hundred times less than it is, its mere existence would still be sufficient to establish a truth that may be expressed in various ways, although always only somewhat indirectly, namely that we have

not to be pleased but rather sorry about the existence of the world; that its non-existence would be preferable to its existence; that it is something which at bottom ought not to be.[29]

According to Schopenhauer, in other words, we should prefer inexistence to existence. We should prefer a world without us to a world with us. We should not be content with ourselves or the world, but should rather be frustrated by them. Schopenhauer's heirs are legion: Albert Camus is one of the most famous. But his view was inherited not only by philosophers. It underlies the outlook of George Bailey from the Christmas classic *It's a Wonderful Life*. Not the George Bailey of the movie's happy ending, but the George Bailey who wishes he had never been born. Once we learn to recognize Schopenhauer's view, we start to see it everywhere. We could call it the Schopenhauer Sulk.[30]

The problem with the Schopenhauer Sulk is not that it neglects human fallenness. The problem, rather, is that the outlook *overemphasizes* human fallenness, and in doing so, neglects the discussion in the first part of this chapter. Recall where we started: the basic equality view. This thesis claims humans are equal and that we are *dignified* in our equality. At the heart of the basic equality view is the idea that humans are good, that we are worth saving, that we are created in the image of God, that existence is better than non-existence. No matter how you phrase it, the basic equality view thus stands opposed to the Schopenhauer Sulk. Embrace basic equality, and you gain a helpful roadmap for respecting the basic equality of all humans. But you also gain an antidote to those views that overemphasize the nastier parts of humanity.

## Striking a Balance

The fallen dignity view of human nature strikes a balance: basic equality on the one hand, an insistence on human fallenness on the other. The first views us through an idealistic lens; the second balances that idealistic outlook with clear-eyed realism. We have seen that both these ideas are explicitly Christian, rooted in the larger Christian story of our place in the cosmos. But you needn't be a Christian to endorse equality and fallenness. In fact, the fallen dignity view borders on being intuitive.

Yet the fallen dignity view is also deeply countercultural. It runs contrary to the assumptions that govern much of our individual and social lives. Basic equality, on the one hand, stands against those views that reduce humans to sets of metrics or cogs in a larger social machine. The idea of human fallenness, on the other, opposes those outlooks that strive to eliminate our limitations through life hacks or curated filters. Basic equality and fallenness may have a ring of truth about them. These theses, however, are near impossible to embrace wholeheartedly, given the cultural tides that pull against them.

Nevertheless, some embrace them. Here we return to the biographical sketches with which I opened this chapter: Saint Mother Teresa and Saint Damien of Molokai. The lives of these saints—and countless others I could have mentioned—strike us as attractive, but as challenging to comprehend. At least at first. Their lives, however, begin to come into focus in the space between basic equality and human fallenness. Basic equality, for Mother Teresa or Damien of Molokai, was not some abstract principle. It was rather a way of life. The lives of these saints would be unintelligible—they would appear unhinged—absent the driving conviction that every life, and especially the lives of the most vulnerable, carries infinite value. Yet saints are human, too. And in being human, saints started out as sinners, navigating their paths to holiness in a world of fellow sinners. Recognizing this does not undermine their sainthood. Rather, it is part of what formed them as saints to begin with. It is this recognition that lies behind the "patience of a saint." Patience with the rest of us, as we slip back into bad habits and old vices and misguided beliefs. And patience with themselves, as they journey on their paths to holiness. In living out basic equality, figures such as Mother Teresa and Damien of Molokai never lost sight of the fact that both they and those whom they served started out in the same place—as sinners.

The balance between equality and fallenness can be difficult to strike. Emphasize fallenness too much, and you'll find yourself shuffling along with the Schopenhauer Sulk. Emphasize equality sans fallenness, and you'll wind up with a caricature of humanity. There is a reason sainthood is rare, and a reason why saints often look so strange. The balance they have found is one that few of us ever manage.

But understanding the saints is not our goal. Our goal is one we have largely set aside: figuring out a path forward when presented with new technologies of human enhancement (remember that problem?!). The trails blazed by the transhumanists and the modern Luddites leave us with unanswered questions, counterintuitive implications, and misleading guidance. The all-out embrace of the transhumanist seems too hasty; the outright rejection of the modern Luddite, hyperbolically negative. We need a middle path.

The fallen dignity view provides just this. A way out of the doldrums. Balance our evaluation of human enhancement with an embrace of basic equality on the one hand, and a nod to human fallenness on the other. Strike that balance right, and we gain an approach that navigates a narrow passage between the excesses of the modern Luddite and the transhumanist. At least that's what I'll be arguing. Let's dive in.

## Chapter 5

# Enhancing Humanity

I'm typing these words on a beat-up Apple computer. Sitting beside the keyboard is a cup of coffee in an insulated mug. I didn't always have a mug like this and spent years drinking lukewarm coffee. Good riddance to that! I'll have another cup around two or three this afternoon, when my night of interrupted sleep (I have three small kids, remember?) catches up with me. Since I mostly work in the morning, the weather is still cool, and I'm wearing a performance fleece jacket, made of some new spin on polyester. When I finish writing, I'll take off the fleece. Then adjust the air conditioning and tuck into breakfast. Usually oatmeal.

Later this week, I'll head into my office. Chicago traffic follows unpredictable patterns, so I use my phone's GPS to navigate. If the Eisenhower expressway jams, Siri will route me elsewhere. Along the way, I will listen to an audio book through my car's Bluetooth hookup. If I plan right, I can finish my reading for class while weaving through the daily commuters and tourists that clog the highways.

After meeting with students—some in-person, others through video chat; some anxious about an upcoming paper, others excited about a new internship opportunity—I'll start teaching. I usually lean on a PowerPoint presentation to structure my classes. After a few hours in the classroom, I head back to my car, power up the audio book, and check with Siri for directions home.

This evening, I'll play a board game, read a stack of books to my kids, help cook dinner, and wash dishes. If I have time, I'll spend a half hour on the elliptical in the basement. Answer emails. Put kids to bed. Say evening prayers. Watch some TV, set my alarm (cringe a little at how few hours there will be before it rings), get into bed. Rinse. Repeat. A day in the life of a twenty-first century philosopher. Not very exciting, it turns out. Fulfilling? Sure. But there won't be any reality TV series (or even any lifestyle blogs) made about it any time soon.

I used a memoir to start this chapter, however, not because the life I lead is particularly interesting. Rather, I used it because I assume my life is quite a bit like yours. At least in one regard. My life is a mixture of enhanced and unenhanced practices. Of beta technologies and perfected designs. Of Siri and performance fleeces and video calls, yes, but also board games and traffic jams and oatmeal. My life interweaves shortcuts and artificial boosts with timeworn technologies. Sometimes it is difficult to separate the two.

Take my coffee habit. Coffee provides an artificial boost. Any way you cut it, a cup of coffee counts as a human enhancement. Yet coffee drinking is not the product of some Silicon Valley startup or overhyped scientific breakthrough. I drink coffee because my dad does, and my grandpa before him. Coffee drinking is an enhancement *and* a traditional practice, a chemical boost *and* an established convention. Take a different example: reading. No, not audio books. Or Kindles. Just plain old reading. As in, *books*. As basic as it gets, you might think. But that wasn't always how people saw it. The philosopher Plato, writing around 400 BC, found writing to be an unnatural boost.[1] He argued that people should rely on their memories to recall a line of poetry or a shopping list. Newfangled tech like pens and paper detract from our ability to memorize and should be avoided. Or so Plato argued. If he was right, technologies of human enhancement are therefore not limited to genetic modification or brain zapping or the latest app on your smart watch. These technologies are instead lined up neatly on your bookshelf.

What's the takeaway? Just this: human enhancement technologies are neither easily identifiable nor separable from our unenhanced lives. Our lives are instead shot through with enhancement. Sometimes, it turns up in expected areas. In the promises of a new startup or in the hallways of a university laboratory. Other times, it pops up in unexpected places: in the clothing we wear; in our morning cup of coffee; in a book read by the evening fire.

These enhancements cannot all be bad for us. We cannot—and should not—aim to eliminate human enhancement from our lives. This conclusion should be obvious when we have reflected on just how pervasive enhancement technologies are. Yet, as we have learned from the modern Luddites, we should also greet new enhancement technologies with suspicion. Human enhancement can chisel away at authenticity and accomplishment, and injustice often lurks in the background of its development.

Where does this leave us? Back where we left off at the end of chapter 3. In particular, back to the idea that the maps charted by the transhumanist and modern Luddite can't be quite right. Human enhancement is not an unmistakable good, as transhumanists claim. But neither is it an unredeemable mistake, as modern Luddites might be tempted to argue.

The fallen dignity view provides a way forward. It can blaze a trail for Christians and non-Christians alike. Start with an understanding of humans as fallen yet dignified and your approach avoids the excesses of the transhumanists and modern Luddites even while retaining their insights. Unlike either the transhumanist or modern Luddite approach, an approach rooted in fallen dignity does not provide easy answers or lines in the sand. Instead, it calls for careful discernment. The lack of a clear-cut vision may be seen by some as a liability. I see it as a value added. The current of human enhancement runs through our lives in subtle ways. Any attempt to navigate through it must be equally subtle.

## Modern Luddites, Meet Fallen Dignity

Recall the modern Luddites. According to them, human enhancement can undermine authenticity, disrupt identity, overstep human limitations, strain our relationships, and perpetuate injustices. That's quite the laundry list of problems, problems we should take seriously.

Not all modern Luddites are Christians, yet their view springs from recognizably Christian sensibilities. Writers such as Wendell Berry—who, if you recall, won't buy a computer—often use recognizably Christian language in their writings. Other Luddites don't mention Christianity but their religious commitments linger in the background, if you know where to look for them. When the President's Council on Bioethics reflects on "the possible hubris in trying to improve upon human nature," you can catch a whiff of Christian influence.[2] As a Christian, I believe Luddites are on target in referencing the Christian tradition to criticize the new, the shiny, and the flashy. Christianity is not new, shiny, or flashy: its teachings are ancient, time-tested, and grounded in tradition.

Modern Luddites also face problems. Yet these problems are surmountable, and I believe the fallen dignity view can help us overcome them. I'll say how in a minute. For now, a teaser-trailer of what I'll be arguing: while modern Luddites correctly identify problematic tendencies in human enhancement, there is a tendency among modern Luddites to focus their criticism on technologies themselves. In doing so, they can miss what is actually disturbing—but also potentially valuable—about these technologies. A better way forward: focus on the ideas of basic equality and human fallenness. Doing so will inevitably deflate the appeal of human enhancement. Your attitude towards it will shift from across-the-board rejection to open-minded indifference. But this is getting ahead of ourselves. Let's back up and tackle the argument from the beginning.

Recall, to start, the credential view. This view says we matter because of some characteristic we have or earn. Faster, stronger, taller, smarter, richer: according to the credential view, these attributes (or something else) make human beings valuable. The basic equality view rejects this picture. While proponents of basic equality don't shy away from human difference, they reject the idea that our buying power or skin color or ability can confer value. Instead, human value is divvied out in equal (and generous) measure to all humans. We matter—and we matter dearly—simply because we are human. Not because of any credential we can show or earn.

Even if the basic equality view resists many currents of modern culture, most of us—Christian and non-Christian alike—agree with it. We are now in a position to see why this matters in the context of our discussion. Put simply: once you have set aside the credential view and embraced basic equality, the appeal of human enhancement deflates. Like an unfiltered Instagram post, the glitz is gone.

To see this, contrast two fictional characters. We'll call them Nora and Mora (*More-a* . . . get it?):

| Nora | Mora |
|---|---|
| Plain old human memory. | Memory has been modified to be razor sharp to and to include mostly good memories. |
| Genes are a gift from mom and dad. | Genes have been crafted in a lab, and include a boost in disease-resistance, increased muscle mass, and a more efficient metabolism. |
| Average (okay, a little less than average) IQ: 85 | IQ pushing 140 due to optogenetics, well-aimed neurostimulation, and some genetic tweaks. |
| Expected to live to seventy "or eighty if strength endures." | Going strong at 75 and could easily reach 130. The secret? Diet, pharmaceuticals, and a range of other techniques. |
| Stuck driving her own car, doing her own taxes, and doing her own research. | Driving? Taxes? Research? There's an algorithm for that. |

What to make of Nora and Mora? At first glance, you may think that Mora's life is *more valuable* than Nora's. That's my initial reaction, at any rate. And I assume it is a common one.

But that's the credential view talking. Sure, there are things about Mora's life that are desirable. Who doesn't want to feel spry at 75? Yet to say that Mora's life is *more valuable* caves to the temptation to see human value as conferred by intelligence or health or ability.

Swap this way of thinking, however, with the basic equality view. The basic equality view delivers a straightforward evaluation: Nora's life matters *just as much* as Mora's. And if there was even more to Mora's life—say, for example, that she becomes the US President or cures cancer or lives to 250—the verdict fails to waver. Why? Both Nora and Mora are equally human, and human value comes from our shared humanity. End of story. So not only does Nora's life matter just as much as Mora's. So, too, *your* life matters just as much as both of theirs. Elon Musk, Barack Obama, a lonely teen in Philadelphia, your Aunt Susan, the guy who picks up your recycling at 3:00 p.m. sharp every Tuesday: each one of these lives is equally valuable, according the basic equality view.

Sit with that idea for a moment. Let it sink in. Stew on it. Because even if you intellectually accept the basic equality view, we rarely view the world through the lens it provides. We rarely live it out. If we did, our lives would look more like those of Mother Teresa and Damien of Molokai. Indeed, as St. Paul might put it, fully endorsing the basic equality view would transform us "by the renewing of [our] minds" (Rom 12:2).

One avenue for this transformation would be in our evaluation of human enhancement. According to the basic equality view, after all, the end goals of human enhancement—longer lives, sharper intellects, healthier bodies—do not make human life matter. Human life matters because it is human life. Full stop. The basic equality view thus entails that a memory-boosted, long-lived, disease-resistant life is *no more valuable* than a life lived in beta. That being boosted and basic are on a par. That an enhanced life is not really "enhanced" after all. In this regard, the modern Luddite get things exactly right: their perspective encourages us to get past the initial excitement over human enhancement and reflect carefully on our values. If we do, we'll see that human enhancement is not all it is cracked up to be. A resilient genetic code or long life or boosted IQ isn't what gives value to our lives. We are *already* valuable. Simply by virtue of being human.

Yet endorsing basic equality does not entail a flat-out rejection of novel enhancements in the way some modern Luddites argue. For notice something crucial: while the basic equality view rejects the credential view wholeheartedly, it does not suggest there is anything wrong with human enhancement *itself*. Yes, our reasons for pursuing it are often misguided, powered by an unreflective ratification of the credential view. Yet rejecting the credential view does not yield the conclusion that human enhancement itself is bad. In fact, there may be other perfectly good reasons to pursue it. A high IQ may not make *you* more valuable, but it can sure come in handy when trying to solve a complicated engineering problem. Likewise, a sharper memory or longer life won't make you matter more than someone without them. Embracing basic equality undermines the credential view—and with it, one of the main propellants motivating our pursuit of human enhancement—but does not undermine human enhancement technology itself.

An analogy might help. Suppose you really want a high-end parka. Like, a *really* high-end parka. Why? You'll admit it: primarily to impress all the wrong people. Flaunt that parka at the right party, and your reputation skyrockets. So you spend hours ogling the company website in your spare time, shuffling funds around to make the purchase happen. Now, a moment's reflection might reveal that your motivation here is misguided. Your mom got it right: if your friends only like you for your parka, they are not your friends. Suppose you recognize this fact and internalize it. Inevitably, your enthusiasm for the parka plummets. But notice something: this doesn't mean the coat *itself* is bad. In fact: you may still need to buy it. After all, you may still need a winter coat. And maybe you have good reason to opt for the high-end one. Maybe it will keep you warmer, last longer, and fit better than the bargain basement variety. So even after you've rejected your initial reasons for wanting the parka, you may still make the purchase. And do so with a clear conscience.

Here's the point: the basic equality view, by undermining the credential view, deflates our estimation of human enhancement. It knocks over the reasons we would typically provide for pursuing it. Yet this does not deliver the conclusion that there is something wrong with human enhancement *itself*, any more then rejecting selfish motives for buying a parka entails there is something wrong with the coat. Like the modern Luddite, an outlook grounded in basic equality eyes human enhancement with suspicion. Yet it does not reject human enhancement across the board, nor does it fix in its crosshairs any particular enhancement technology.

This feature is crucial, as it is what allows us to avoid the problems faced by modern Luddites, at least those who would insist on applying Luddite concerns consistently. For recall the problems faced by the modern Luddites. Most centrally, they must contend with the parity principle, which says two things should be treated as morally equivalent unless we can identity something morally wrong with one but not the other. So, for example, if we affirm coffee drinking as perfectly fine but reject neural stimulation as morally problematic, we had better find a good moral reason to give coffee a thumbs up and neural stimulation the boot. If we can't find such a reason and still treat the two differently, our moral behavior is inconsistent. The parity principle thus creates problems for modern Luddites who would reject modern enhancements across the board. It isn't clear, after all, that there are moral differences between new enhancement technologies and the technologies we already embrace.

An approach grounded in basic equality, however, does not face this problem. We have already seen the reason: this approach does not throw human enhancement technologies to the curb, but instead invites us to reflect on our motives for pursuing them. While the parity principle challenges us to defend the morality of choosing those technologies, an approach grounded in basic equality avoids having to take a defensive posture. True, the approach often deflates our assessment of novel technologies. Because it emphasizes that a smarter-faster-stronger-younger version of you is no more valuable than the version staring out at you from the mirror every morning, the approach reduces the pull that human enhancement has on us. Once we've internalized basic equality, the prospect of an artificially-long, memory-boosted, genetically refined life simply doesn't strike us as the obvious goal we should be pursuing. This kind of life—while perhaps practically helpful in some ways—is no more valuable than the life we are currently living. Yet in taking this stance, we haven't staked out any moral turf we have to defend. Generally, the basic equality view pushes us to reflect on our reasons for pursuing human enhancement rather than reject any particular technology.

The fallen dignity view, however, is not exhausted by basic equality. The fallen dignity view claims not only that humans have inherent dignity, but also that we are fallen. And taking fallenness seriously offers further protection from the problematic excesses that modern Luddites may be tempted to defend.

To see why, consider an analogy: suppose you and I stroll into a guitar store. We head directly to the well-polished row of instruments, where I pick up a Les Paul and start strumming some classic rock riffs. The result? A tune that is decidedly not a classic. "Must be the guitar," I pronounce, and move on the Telecasters, where I pick out an ungroovy country rock tune. "Cheap instrument," I explain, and head over to the semi-hollows, where I strum some non-jazzy jazz tunes. Without a hitch in my step, I then proceed to move down the line, picking, tapping, strumming, and plucking one arhythmic mess after another. At each stop, the guitar gets the blame, and you turn yet a deeper shade of red.

What's going on here? Clearly (as the eye-rolling store employees will tell you), I have misidentified the problem. Set on blaming the guitars, I have missed what is obvious to everyone else: that I am the problem. That a better instrument isn't going to solve anything. That the solution depends on a change in *me*: a better sense of rhythm or at least the humility to recognize where the problem lies.

Modern Luddites who insist on the ills of enhancement often stumble in a similar way. By directing their criticism at *the technology*, they fail to appreciate where the real problem lies: with ourselves. Modern Luddites accurately identify many of the problems of human enhancement. Does life extension smack of human hubris? Does genetic engineering often grow from a misplaced vision of what makes human life valuable? Can cognitive enhancement undermine authentic human action? Absolutely. Yet humans have always exhibited hubris and pursued problematic goals. The following passage from Genesis describes the Tower of Babel, but with a few nouns swapped out here and there, could easily describe many of the projects described in this book:

> And they said to one another, "Come, let us make bricks, and burn them thoroughly." And they had brick for stone, and bitumen for mortar. Then they said, "Come, let us build ourselves a city, and a tower with its top in the heavens, and let us make a

name for ourselves; otherwise we shall be scattered abroad upon the face of the whole earth." (Gn 11: 3-4)

Are projects of human enhancement often akin to a kind of Babel? Yes, and that's what modern Luddites get right. Yet abandoning our pursuit of genetic engineering, memory modification, life extension, and the rest won't return us to Eden. Because the problems that our technologies surface are ultimately problems of the human heart. The perils of pursuing perfection will always be with us. With or without new technologies of human enhancement.

And this is, of course, precisely the idea behind fallenness: the idea that, as Chesterton had it, *we* are the problem with the world. That all the ills around us—often sketched in abstract and impersonal terms—can trace their lineage to a problem of the human heart. The upshot: an impersonalized account that locates the root cause of a problem in a technology can never be quite right. The strategy instead distracts us from the root of the problem. Modern Luddites who shun enhancement technology often fall into just this trap. By pinning their criticism on enhancement technology *itself*, they miss the insights of both basic equality and human fallenness. Emphasize those views before evaluating enhancement technology, however, and we can take on board the insights of modern Luddites even while avoiding the excesses of luddism gone awry.

## Transhumanists and Fallen Dignity

Transhumanists, recall, occupy territory directly opposite the modern Luddites. While modern Luddites face the temptation to throw new enhancement technologies to the curb, transhumanists embrace these same technologies with open arms. While Luddites eye new technologies with suspicion, transhumanists eye them like a kid in a candy shop. While Luddites see genetic enhancement and life extension and artificial intelligence as undermining our humanity, trans-humanists see these technologies as opening new avenues for human potential. Transhumanists, in short, love what modern Luddites hate and hate what modern Luddites love. Our question here: how does transhumanism stack up against the fallen dignity view?

Some have attempted to bring the two closer together by arguing that aspects of transhumanism intersect with Christianity. I hope it is clear by now that this project faces an uphill battle. Yet it isn't entirely quixotic. In the Gospel of John, for example, Christ says, "I came that they may have life, and have it abundantly" (Jn 10:10). That has a transhu-manist ring to it. The Christian Transhumanist Association, moreover, dedicates itself to merging transhumanism with Christianity, and advocates for the following string of Christian-flavored ideals:

1. **We believe that God's mission involves the transformation and renewal of creation** including humanity, and that we are called by Christ to participate in that mission: working against illness, hunger, oppression, injustice, and death.

2. **We seek growth and progress along every dimension of our humanity:** spiritual, physical, emotional, mental—and at all levels: individual, community, society, world.

3. **We recognize science and technology as tangible expressions of our God-given impulse to explore and discover** and as a natural outgrowth of being created in the image of God.

4. **We are guided by Jesus' greatest commands** to "Love the Lord your God with all your heart, soul,

mind, and strength . . . and love your neighbor as yourself."

5. **We believe that the intentional use of technology, coupled with following Christ, can empower us to grow into our identity** as humans made in the image of God.[3]

These ideals may be vague (more on that in a second) but there's no denying that the Christian Transhumanists find some points of contact between the traditions.

At the more academic end of things, scholars have also aimed to close gaps between transhumanism and Christianity. Micah Redding, Executive Director of the Christian Transhumanist Association, has argued that our status as being made in the image and likeness of God "evokes a powerful vision of its transcendent potential."[4] Likewise, Redding argues, transhumanists and Christians both believe that "death was not an inevitable reality to be accepted" and that the world's ultimate future is one of "springing forth into vibrant new life."[5] Reformed Theologian Ronald Cole-Turner also sees Christianity and transhumanism as being in productive dialogue: "The futuristic scenarios of the transhumanists are an open invitation for the church to think its own way about the culture of the future"[6] And Bible Professor J.M. Strahan points out areas where Christianity and transhumanism seem to explicitly overlap: both aim to alleviate suffering; both advocate for ethical principles such as loving others; both "regard humanity as neither wholly virtuous nor wholly vicious."[7]

What to make of these observations? I'll show my cards: while Christian Transhumanists may demonstrate that Christianity and transhumanism are not entirely at odds, I'm underwhelmed by the case they make. Are there points of overlap between Christianity and transhumanism? Sure. But zoom out far enough, and *any* two positions will appear close together. On a map of the world, Pittsburgh and Chicago look like neighbors, but anyone who has spent a day on the Ohio turnpike will tell you that the two are separated by scores of miles. The lesson: whether two positions are "close" is a matter of perspective. And by my lights, you must zoom out pretty far to see the overlap between Christianity and transhumanism. Is it true that both transhumanists and Christians work against hunger, oppression, and death? That both aim for personal growth? That both find it laudable to love others? That both believe in the intentional use of technology? That both view human morality as a mixed bag? That both refuse to see death as an inevitable end? Sure. But scores of other schools of thought do as well. I would hazard to say that *most* schools of thought are on the same page here. Finding common ground between Christianity and transhumanism requires taking a sweeping perspective and shuffling the details to the bottom of the deck.

I'm not the first to notice that Christianity and transhumanism are uneasy bedfellows. On the transhumanist side, in his "The Fable of the Dragon Tyrant," Nick Bostrom ridicules religion as antithetical to transhumanist goals.[8] And scripture does not tell us merely that we should live more abundantly: it also says that "the last will be first and first will be last" (Mt 20:16). That doesn't sound very transhumanist at all. Start noticing the details, and Christianity and transhumanism start to look different indeed.

So where do the Christian Transhumanists go wrong? My diagnosis: while cherry-picking superficial similarities between Christianity and transhumanism, they ignore the deeper ways in which the fallen dignity view clashes with transhumanist ideals. Dwell with either basic equality or human fallenness and you'll drift away from transhumanism. More than that: you'll find a position that can accommodate the strengths of transhumanism even while avoiding its excesses.

To see this, recall the basic dilemma facing transhumanists. If they lean into the transhumanist life as objectively valuable, they take on board problematic assumptions. If you say that a longer life or higher IQ or certain genetic markers make a human worth more, you are committed to saying that some humans matter more than others. That the more someone can do or longer someone lives, the more valuable someone is. That human worth is not grounded on our fundamental dignity, but on the contingent abilities we possess (or don't). In chapter 2, we labeled this way of thinking ableism. Clunky name, yes. Yet most of us (including most transhumanists) want to avoid it.

Yet if transhumanists dodge ableism by rejecting the idea of enhancement as objectively valuable, it isn't clear why we should pursue their projects to begin with. That's the other horn of the dilemma transhumanists face. Yes, transhumanists can avoid ableism: instead of endorsing human enhancement as objectively good, they can instead endorse it as one good among many. But in this case, it isn't clear why we should elevate transhumanist goals above the others we want to pursue. Worse than that: if transhumanist goods offer only cheap thrills—if they don't offer anything of substance—our pursuit of them will inevitably bottom out in despair. Ableism or despair. Quite the dilemma.

The fallen dignity view, however, provides a map for charting a course between those horns. Consider again the idea behind basic equality. This idea closes off the first horn of the transhumanist's dilemma. Basic equality, after all, explicitly rejects the idea that human value is conferred by any credential. Age, ability, IQ: none of these (or any other attribute you'd care to list) give human beings our value. Instead, human value is conferred by our humanity alone.

This much is crystal clear: embrace basic equality, and the threat of ableism dissolves. So much for the first horn of the transhumanist's dilemma.

Proponents of fallen dignity likewise don't face the threat of despair, though it is a bit less clear why this is true. For example, consider human fallenness. As we have seen, the idea behind human fallenness is that humans are sinners, that we have fallen from grace, that we are imperfect. You can put a more or less theological gloss on our fallenness, yet the basic idea here is both simple and uncontroversial: we cannot save ourselves from ourselves. Initially, this may seem to smack of despair. Not the world-weary despair of the transhumanist, but rather the kind that comes from ruminating on the human condition.

I'll admit it: on its own, the idea of human fallenness may lead to this conclusion. Recall the Schopenhauer Sulk, according to which "non-existence would be preferable to its existence." Yet the fallen dignity view—*taken as a whole*—actively resists the Schopenhauer Sulk. It does so by balancing human fallenness with a steadfast commitment to basic equality. And at the heart of the basic equality view is the idea that humans are good, that we are worth saving, that existence is better than non-existence. Embrace the full picture presented by the fallen dignity view, and you gain an escape route from despair. The dignity of humans is sufficient to overcome that threat.

The fallen dignity view thus avoids both ableism and despair, threading the needle between the transhumanist's unattractive options. In doing so, it also changes our perspective on human enhancement technologies themselves. For the transhumanist, enhancement technologies—from life boosting drugs to CRISPR-Cas9-fueled genetic tweaking to memory-altering brain zaps—are either a surefire path for transcending humanity, or else a playground for moral exploration. Proponents of fallen dignity, by contrast, don't aspire to transcend our humanity to begin with, and so don't view enhancement technologies as a means to do so. The fallen dignity view, in fact, doesn't say much at all about enhancement technologies. It instead asks us to reflect more carefully on *ourselves*: on our dignity and our fallenness.

## Modern Luddites and Transhumanists: Bedazzled by Technology

At first glance, the modern Luddites and transhumanists couldn't be more different. The Luddites, donned in tweed blazers, shaking their fists at novel enhancement technologies, pen cranky manifestos from lonely lake cabins, pining for a return to pen and paper (or maybe even quill and parchment). The transhumanists, meanwhile, sporting black turtlenecks and skinny jeans, jot blog posts from their modernist homes, welcoming these same new technologies with open arms.

The differences are indeed stark. Yet our discussion suggests the two groups share one key feature: both fall into problems precisely when they become bedazzled by modern technological enhancements, embracing or rejecting novel technologies primarily because they are new. Both camps, we have seen, go wrong when they focus their attention primarily on the perils and promises of enhancement technology *itself*.

Ethically speaking, however, this is never a solid way to proceed. New technologies and possibilities, after all, are not delivered to us in a moral vacuum. They are instead presented in a context where we *already* pursue goals and deem things valuable. Modern Luddites and transhumanists both face the same temptation: to get stunned by the sparkle of what could be, and in doing so, forget to reflect on what has been.

That's why fallen dignity stands out, and why it has an advantage over both approaches. As we have seen, the fallen dignity view does not start with an evaluation of modern enhancement technology itself. It instead asks us to reflect on ourselves as both infinitely dignified and inevitably fallen, and only then turns to scrutinize anything outside ourselves.

Of course, there may be some applications of enhancement technologies that fallen dignity takes a clear stance on. Consider: genetic engineering motivated by racist goals—for example, aiming to erase a certain set of characteristics from the gene pool—is a clear violation of basic equality, and so won't get the go-ahead from the fallen dignity view. Likewise, certain methods used in genetic engineering—such as problematic uses of human embryos—may be a direct violation of basic equality. Notice, though, that even here the problem is not with the technology itself, but the way in which we are using it. That's characteristic of the response by fallen dignity: to look beyond the technology itself and ground our analysis in a larger system of values.

Yet a frustrating question remains: how *precisely* can we use the fallen dignity view to navigate the brave new world that lies before us? At least transhumanists and modern Luddites have this advantage: their take is clear. Stark, even. You needn't guess what the modern Luddites' or transhumanists' take on CRISPR-Cas9 or memory modification or life extension is. They tell you up front.

The fallen dignity view is not like this. As we have seen, fallen dignity leads us to eye new technologies with suspicion, yet avoids rejecting them outright. Likewise, with transhumanism, fallen dignity acknowledges the advantages of new discoveries, but refuses to elevate these discoveries unnecessarily.

Viewed one way, this middle-of-the-road evaluation gives proponents of fallen dignity a theoretical advantage over the hyperbolic assessments that are sometimes delivered by modern Luddites and transhumanists. Viewed a different way, however, the evaluation may seem wishy-washy. Milquetoast. Lukewarm. And no one likes a waffler. This challenge—we'll call it the Wishy-Washy Worry—is where we turn in the closing pages.

Conclusion

# Enhancement and the Good Life

I don't know about you, but I can be tempted by a well-drawn line in the sand. One that demarcates "my people" from "their people." My politics from theirs. The right take on morality from a legion of warped versions. Life is messy, like a beach cluttered with refuse and battered by tides. Clear lines in the sand help us orient ourselves.

The problem with lines in the sand, of course, is that sand shifts. The wind blows it away and erodes it. The tide comes in and erases it entirely. Or, on closer inspection, we discover that we drew the line in the wrong place to begin with. I may endorse a consistently pro-life ethic . . . and find this leaves me lost in the contemporary political landscape. I may consistently attend religious services . . . but find more common ground with a group of atheists than my fellow parishioners. Lines in the sand may provide comfort. But they are exceedingly difficult to maintain.

This outlook, we have seen, is characteristic of the fallen dignity view's approach to human enhancement. The fallen dignity view gains an advantage over modern Luddites and transhumanists precisely by refusing to draw any line in the sand. It refuses to demonize or valorize novel enhancement technologies, choosing instead to turn our reflection inward: on *ourselves* as fallen yet infinitely dignified. Start with that, internalize it, understand it, and live by it. From there, the importance of enhancement technologies fades into the background.

Well, that's fine and good, you might think. But what to do when we are confronted with novel technologies? When given the opportunity to zap our brains or tweak our genes or lengthen our lives? Or, for that matter, when deciding whether to delete our social media accounts or swap a tablet for pen and paper or a well-worn wool sweater for a new performance fleece? Considered academically and from a distance, the fallen dignity view has its advantages. But when we are faced with real-world decisions and challenges, the theory may seem frustrating. In refusing to draw any lines it the sand, it may seem as if its proponents are attempting to have their cake and eat it too. And that won't do. We are, after all, *even now* faced with questions about modern enhancement technologies, questions that will only gain momentum in the coming decades.

This way of restating the Wishy-Washy Worry, the objection that the fallen dignity view is so indecisive that it really doesn't provide guidance. An important objection, since enhancement technologies present us with concrete issues and questions that we must address in concrete (not abstract or merely theoretical) ways. To answer it, we turn to an unexpected place. Not to the startups of Silicon Valley or a Reddit thread or even a lonely cabin in the woods. Instead, we turn to Basque country. Over five hundred years ago. And to a man named Ignatius.

Ignatius of Loyola began life as a soldier, proud of his good looks and enamored with tales of chivalry. After a cannonball shattered his leg, however, Ignatius decided to shift course in life. Rather than pursuing a career at court, he would instead aim for sainthood. Not the kind of guy who does things halfheartedly, Ignatius achieved his goal—he was canonized in 1622, just sixty-six years after his death. Today, St. Ignatius's legacy lives on in the order of religious brothers and priests he founded (the Jesuits) and in their many institutions around the globe. You may have heard of some of them: Georgetown University, Saint Louis University, Fordham University, and my own home institution, Loyola University in Chicago. Alongside those universities, the Jesuits run a slew of high schools across the United States and across the world. More important than these institutions, however, Ignatius left us with the *Spiritual Exercises*, a guide that has proven foundational for spiritual growth and direction.

The *Spiritual Exercises* contain many insights. Here, we'll focus on his idea of *indifference*. In a section of the *Spiritual Exercises* called The Principle and Foundation, Ignatius introduces the idea:

> The human person is created to praise, reverence, and serve God Our Lord, and by so doing to save his or her soul. . . . It follows from this that one must use other created things in so far as they help towards one's end, and free oneself from them in so far as they are obstacles to one's end. To do this we need to make ourselves indifferent to all created things, provided the matter is subject to our free choice and there is no prohibition. Thus as far as we are concerned, we should not want health more than illness, wealth more than poverty, fame more than disgrace, a long life more than a short one, and similarly for all the rest, but we should desire and choose only what helps us more towards the end for which we are created.[1]

Skimmed quickly, the passage could be read as endorsing a dismissive attitude. One that says we shouldn't care about much at all—not even about whether we are sick or poor or live a short life. The Wishy-Washy Worry all over again.

But that's not right. For Ignatius, to be indifferent is not to fail to care. It is rather to keep our eyes set on what is good, on what is *ultimately* good for us, and then to organize our lives around this. For Ignatius, the ultimate good is "to praise, reverence, and serve God." So, if a healthy life helps me praise, reverence, and serve God, Ignatius would say, "so be it." But if a life of sickness serves that goal better, we should embrace sickness instead. If wealth can bring us closer to God, bring on the cash. But if poverty does the trick, skip the hedge fund. In short: through the concept of indifference, Ignatius urges us to live a life of consistency, bringing our day-to-day desires and goals in line with what is ultimately good for us. If we have identified what is truly good for us, organizing our lives around it will by definition guide us to a good life.

So what is a good human life exactly? An excellent question, one that has been central to the history of philosophy. Entire sections of libraries are devoted to it. Entire libraries are devoted to it, for that matter.[2] If I attempted to answer it in a slim book's conclusion, I would be laughed out of the academy.

Yet our discussion has hinted at ways *not* to answer the question, has shown that many of the goals of human enhancement—a long life, boosted intelligence, razor-sharp memory—cannot be crucial to a truly good human life. Why? Because, we have seen, the good things human enhancement can provide always come with an asterisk. A long life can be good. But it can also warp into the stuff of nightmares. Intelligence can be good. But to overemphasize intelligence (or any other ability) lands us in the muck of ableism. The goods promised by human enhancement, in short, can be good. But only conditionally so. They are good *only if* they are put into service of some higher or more basic good.

Ignatius, we have seen, identifies this ultimate good as a life in which we can "praise, reverence, and serve God." If you are a Christian, you probably agree with Ignatius (or something in the ballpark). If you are not a Christian, you may not agree. Either way, I would encourage you to reflect on what is good—*truly good*—for your life. What ultimately gives it meaning? What deserves your worship? What should be the focal point of your pursuits, desires, and goals? Then, after you've answered these questions, orient your life around the answers you give. *That* is the spirit of Ignatian indifference.

For example, imagine asking Ignatius whether you should buy a new house or start an intense exercise program or accept a prestigious award. He would not just say "yes" or "no," but would urge you to reflect on whether these things move you closer to the service and praise of God, or further away. Put in more general terms, he would not provide a simple answer, but would instead challenge you to reflect on whether these courses of actions would be good—truly good—for you. Whether they would move you closer to a good life, or further away from it.

Wishy-washy? Seemingly so. But look closer. Ignatius's response, in fact, has real bite, even outside the realm of human enhancement. Tempted to purchase a larger house or build your following on social media or climb the ladder at work? It's *possible* that these things could be in service of what is ultimately good for us. But the likelihood is low. From a Christian perspective, it is the poor and meek that are blessed, not the social media influencers with sprawling suburban mansions. And even if you are not a Christian, our discussion in this book has made it clear that the bigger, the flashier, the shinier, and the newer are not synonymous with a good human life. The lesson? A consistent focus on what is good for humans often subverts the decision-making rubrics that have been handed to us. If you laser-focus on what is truly good for you, your decisions will often pull against the cultural tides. They may look radical, even incomprehensible to those around you.

In addressing the Wishy-Washy Worry, we can therefore take a cue from this way of thinking. When confronted with novel enhancement technologies, we must determine whether these technologies are in fact good for us, whether they move us closer to or further away from a well-lived life. That's the spirit of Ignatian indifference. And it is one that leads us to the view we have arrived at in our discussion, a view in which the hyperbolic arguments of both the modern Luddites and transhumanists are deflated and replaced with careful reflection on what precisely enhancement technologies help us achieve. Should I zap my brain for some extra IQ? Try out a new life-extending technology? Buy a VR headset and enter the metaverse? Swap my pen and paper for a smartphone or laptop? From Ignatius's perspective, we can't answer these questions without first answering the more basic question about how these technologies help us or hinder us in living a truly good life.

Wishy washy? Far from it. The response, once more, has real bite. Tempted to zap your brain or edit your child's genome or live life in the metaverse or scroll social media or outsource your tasks to artificial intelligence or boost your life expectancy? It is *possible* that these things could contribute to a good life. But it's not terribly likely either. Just as a life grounded in indifference will resist the materialistic and self-focused forces of contemporary society, so too it will dismiss many forms of human enhancement as distracting from our ultimate aims. An indifferent life will inevitably resist the ebb and flow of modern society.

The whole point of indifference, in fact, is to ground your life in values that lie outside that ebb and flow.

And that's why Ignatius's strategy works just as well today as it worked five hundred years ago. Humans have always been distracted by the new, the glitzy, the hyped. We have, for that matter, always been distracted by things that, on closer reflection, we know are not the crucial ingredients to a good life. Humans have always aimed to build Babel, even when we knew that ultimately would do us no good. We have always been tempted by the perils of perfection.

How to avoid the distinctive perils presented by novel enhancement technologies? The answer we have arrived at: recognize that they are not distinctive after all. That novel enhancement technologies present us with the same kinds of empty promises—yet also the same kinds of possibilities—that new technological innovations have always presented. By recognizing this, we can avoid hyperbolic reactions and begin reflecting on what ultimately makes a good human life. How to avoid the perils of perfection? Skip perfection. Aim for the good.

# Acknowledgements

This book isn't perfect, but the help I received on it comes close. Thanks to Charlie Camosy, Tom Masters, Greg Metzger, and the team at New City Press for their support, editing, and camaraderie in bringing the book across the finish line. Thanks to Ryan Kemp, Greg Lynch, and Adam Wood for reading drafts of the book, and providing crucial feedback. Thanks to my students, who endured lessons, units, and even an entire course on the themes and arguments found in this book. Thanks to my parents for their support throughout the years. Thanks also to Michael Burns, not only for titling the book, but also for keeping me honest while grappling with the science throughout it. Thanks most of all to my wife, Kelsey, for her support. The book wouldn't have happened without her.

# Notes

## Introduction

1. *www.nueralink.com.*

2. *www.nueralink.com.*

3. Tad Friend, "Silicon Valley's Quest to Live Forever," *The New Yorker,* April 3, 2017.

4. For a thorough discussion of immortalists and healthspanners, see Friend, "Silicon Valley's Quest to Live Forever."

5. *www.alkahest.com.*

6. Ironically, immortalists and healthspanner companies tend to be ephemeral. No doubt some of my discussion in these paragraphs is out-of-date, no matter when you are reading it.

7. Ruairidh Battleday Anna-Katherine Brem, "Modafinil for Cognitive Neuroenhancement in Healthy Non-Sleep-Deprived Subjects: A Systematic Review," *European Neuropsychopharmacology* 25, 11 (2015): 1865-1881.

8. K. Graff Low & A. E. Gendaszek, "Illicit Use of Psychostimulants among College Students: A Preliminary Study," *Psychology, Health & Medicine* 7, 3 (2002): 283-287.

9. Sean McCabe, et al., "Non-Medical Use of Prescription Stimulants among US College Students: Prevalence and Correlates from a National Survey," *Addiction* 100, 1 (2005): 96-106.

10. The passing reference to *Brave New World* is intentional. Aldous Huxley's novel paints a dystopian world in which the central characters use all manner of human enhancement. I highly recommend it as a companion reading to this book.

## Chapter 1
## New Technologies of Human Enhancement

1. Eric Juengst and Daniel Moseley, "Human Enhancement," in *The Stanford Encyclopedia of Philosophy* (Summer 2019 Edition), ed.

Edward N. Zalta, *plato.stanford.edu/archives/sum2019/entries/enhancement/*.

2. Aristotle, *The Complete Works of Aristotle: The Revised Oxford Translation*, ed. Jonathan Barnes (Princeton N.J: Princeton University Press, 1984). See, for example, *Nicomachean Ethics*, 1106b7.

3. See *www.olympics.com*.

4. Larry Cahill, et al., "Beta-Adrenergic Activation and Memory for Emotional Events," *Nature* 371 (1994): 702–704.

5. Merel Kindt, et al., "Beyond Extinction: Erasing Human Fear Responses and Preventing the Return of Fear," *Nature Neuroscience* 12 (2009): 256–258

6. Alain Brunet, et al., "Effect of Post-Retrieval Propanolol on Psychophysiologic Responding During Subsequent Script-Driven Traumatic Imagery in Post-Traumatic Stress Disorder," *Journal of Psychiatric Research* 42 (2008): 503–506.

7. Thomas Giustino et al., "Revisiting Propranolol and PTSD: Memory Erasure or Extinction Enhancement?," *Neurobiology of Learning and Memory* 130 (2016): 26-33.

8. The literature on CRISPR-Cas9 is massive, on both the scientific and ethical sides. To ease into the subject, I recommend Walter Isaacson, *The Code Breaker: Jennifer Doudna, Gene Editing, and the Future of the Human Race* (New York: Simon and Schuster, 2021).

9. Sorry to disappoint fans of *The Chronicles of Narnia*, but you won't be swapping stories with Reepicheep's cousin anytime soon.

10. Thanks to Tom Masters for the suggested use of "supermurine." A new addition to my vocabulary! Maybe, a new addition to yours as well.

11. Christiane Schreiweis, et al., "Humanized Foxp2 Accelerates Learning by Enhancing Transitions from Declarative to Procedural Performance," *Proceedings of the National Academy of Sciences of the United States of America* 111, 39 (2014): 14253-14258.

12. Kathleen Vohs, et al., "The Psychological Consequences of Money," *Science* 314, 5802 (2006): 1154-1156.

13. Shai Danziger, et al., "Extraneous Factors in Judicial Decisions," *Proceedings of the National Academy of Sciences* 108, 17 (2011): 6889-6892.

14. Daniel Kahneman, *Thinking Fast and Slow* (New York: Farrar, Straus, and Giroux, 2011).

15. See, for example, Sana Inoue and Tetsuro Matsuzawa, "Working Memory of Numerals in Chimpanzees," *Current Biology* 17, 23 (2007): 1004-1005.

16. Jane Wang, et al., "Targeted Enhancement of Cortical-Hippocampal Brain Networks and Associative Memory," *Science* 345 (2014): 1054-1057.

17. Adam Green, et al., "Thinking Cap Plus Thinking Zap: tDCS of Frontopolar Cortex Improves Creative Analogical Reasoning and Facilitates Conscious Augmentation of State Creativity in Verb Generation," *Cerebral Cortex* 27, 4 (2017): 2628–2639.

18. Ruairidh Battleday Anna-Katherine Brem, "Modafinil for Cognitive Neuroenhancement in Healthy Non-Sleep-Deprived Subjects: A Systematic Review," *European Neuropsychopharmacology* 25, 11 (2015): 1865-1881.

19. For an accessible discussion, see John Colapinto, "Lighting the Brain," *The New Yorker*, May 18, 2015. For a more technical discussion of the application of optogenetics to human enhancement—specifically, to memory modification—see Przemysław Zawadzki and Agnieszka K Adamczyk, "Personality and Authenticity in Light of the Memory-Modifying Potential of Optogenetics," *American Journal of Bioethics: Neuroscience* 12, 1 (2021): 3-21.

20. Nikolaos Karalis, et al., "4-Hz Oscillations Synchronize Prefrontal-Amygdala Circuits During Fear Behavior," *Nature Neuroscience* 19, 4 (2016): 605-612.

21. Victor Hernandez, et al., "Optogenetic Stimulation of the Auditory Pathway," *The Journal of Clinical Investigation* 124, 3 (2014): 1114-1129.

22. Gillian Matthews, et al., "Dorsal Raphe Dopamine Neurons Represent the Experience of Social Isolation," *Cell* 164, 4 (2016): 617-631.

23. Elizabeth Arias, et al., "Provisional Life Expectancy Estimates for 2021," report number 23 (2022). See *www.cdc.gov/nchs/products/index.htm*.

24. For an excellent—if a bit unconventional—retelling of the myth, see Stephen Fry, *Mythos* (San Francisco: Chronicle Books, 2017), 256-260.

25. United Nations: Department of Economic and Social Affairs, Population Division, "World Population Prospects Highlights," (New York: United Nations, 2019).

26. Khushwant Bhullar and Basil P Hubbard, "Lifespan and Healthspan Extension by Resveratrol," *Biochimica et Biophysica Acta* 1852, 6 (2015): 1209-1218.

27. Richard Weindruch and Roy Walford, "Dietary Restriction in Mice Beginning at 1 Year of Age: Effect on Life-Span and Spontaneous Cancer Incidence," *Science* 215, 4538 (1982): 1415-1418.

28. For more on Churchill, the classic, three-volume biography *The Last Lion* by William Manchester and Paul Reid is the standard. But

*Churchill: Walking with Destiny* by Andrew Roberts is a fine one-volume biography for those wishing to skip the three-volume commitment.

29. Linda Partridge, Matias Fuentealba, and Brian K. Kennedy, "The Quest to Slow Ageing through Drug Discovery," *Nature Reviews Drug Discovery* 19 (2020): 513-532.

30. Filipe Cabreiro, et al., "Metformin Retards Aging in C. elegans by Altering Microbial Folate and Methionine Metabolism," *Cell* 153, 1 (2013): 228-239.

31. Partridge, Fuentealba, and Kennedy, "The Quest to Slow Ageing through Drug Discovery."

Chapter 2
## Humanity+

1. Raffi Katchadourian, "The Doomsday Invention," *The New Yorker*, November 23, 2015.

2. See *www.fhi.ox.ac.uk*.

3. A quick Google search will turn up both. One advantage of transhumanism's techno-utopian outlook is that its adherents often make resources readily available online.

4. Nick Bostrum, "Transhumanist Values," *Journal of Philosophical Research* 30, Issue Supplement (2005): 3-4.

5. David Chalmers, *Reality+* (New York: Norton, 2022), xii.

6. Bostrum, "Transhumanist Values," 3-4.

7. J.R.R. Tolkien, "From a Letter by J.R.R. Tolkien to Milton Waldman, 1951," in *The Silmarillion* (New York: Houghton Mifflin, 2004), *xxvi* (footnote).

8. J.K. Rowling, *Harry Potter and the Sorcerer's Stone* (New York: Bloomsbury Publishing, Illustrated Edition, 2015), 237.

9. The President's Council on Bioethics, *Beyond Therapy: Biotechnology and the Pursuit of Happiness* (Washington DC: The President's Council on Bioethics, 2003), 184.

10. President's Council, *Beyond Therapy*, 184.

11. See especially President's Council, *Beyond Therapy*, 190-192.

12. Bostrum, "Transhumanist Values," 10.

13. Bostrum, "Transhumanist Values," 10.

14. Bostrum, "Transhumanist Values," 12.

15. Bostrum, "Transhumanist Values," 13.

16. Bostrum, "Transhumanist Values," 8.

17. Bostrum, "Transhumanist Values," 8.

18. Bostrum, "Transhumanist Values," 9.

19. The arguments in this paragraph and those preceding it take some inspiration from Colin McGinn, *The Problem of Consciousness* (Cambridge: Blackwell, 1991). McGinn argues that consciousness is mysterious to humans because it outstrips our comprehension. His argument thus parallels the discussions I have given about the way human art might outstrip a dog's comprehension, and the way transhumanist values might outstrip current human comprehension.

20. Bostrum, "Transhumanist Values," 8.

21. Kierkegaard, Soren, *Either/Or: A Fragment of Life*, trans. by Alastair Hannay (New York: Penguin, 2004), 223-241.

22. Kierkegaard, *Either/Or*, 43.

23. Jean-Paul Sartre, "Existentialism is a Humanism," in *Existentialism is a Humanism* (New Haven: Yale University Press, 2007), 22.

Chapter 3
## Luddism Modernized

1. For up-to-date records, see *www.baseball-almanac.com/hitting/hihr4.shtml*

2. Tyler Kepner, "Mark McGwire Admits that He Used Steroids," *The New York Times*, January 11, 2010.

3. Michael S. Schmidt, "Sosa is Said to Have Tested Positive in 2003," *The New York Times*, June 16, 2009.

4. See, for example, Michael Powell, "For Barry Bonds, a Decade of Inflated Blame for the Steroid Era," *The New York Times*, October 20, 2014.

5. For one account of the Luddite movement, see Kirkpatrick Sale, *Rebels Against the Future* (Cambridge, MA: Perseus Publishing, 1996).

6. Jean-Paul Sartre, *Being and Nothingness*, trans. by Hazel E. Barnes (London: Methuen and Co. Ltd, UP Paperback, 1969), 59.

7. Jean-Paul Sartre, *Being and Nothingness*, Part 1, Chapter 2.

8.  Joseph Vukov, "Enduring Questions and the Ethics of Memory Blunting," *Journal of the American Philosophical Association* 3, 2 (2017): 231.

9.  Joseph Vukov, "Enduring Questions...," 231.

10. Thanks to Kimberly Vargas Barreto for helping me think through the limitations of authenticity.

11. President's Council, *Beyond Therapy*, 291-293.

12. Quoted in Sara Goering, et al., "Staying in the Loop: Relational Agency and Identity in Next-Generation DBS for Psychiatry," AJOB *Neuroscience* 8, 2 (2017): 59-70, see page 63.

13. President's Council, *Beyond Therapy*, 291.

14. Michael Sandel, *The Case Against Perfection* (Cambridge, MA: Belnap Press of Harvard University Press, 2007).

15. See, for example, Bishop Robert Barron, *Arguing Religion: A Bishop Speaks at Facebook and Google* (Park Ridge, IL: Word on Fire, 2018), 105-106.

16. Leon Kass, "Ageless Bodies, Happy Souls: Biotechnology and the Pursuit of Perfection," *The New Atlantis* 1 (2003): 9-28.

17. Eric Lander, et al., "Adopt a Moratorium on Heritable Genome Editing," *Nature* 567, 7747 (2019): 165-168.

18. Let me recommend again Stephen Fry's retelling of the Greek myths in his book *Mythos* (San Francisco: Chronicle Books, 2017). The audio version is excellent.

19. Bishop Robert Barron, *Arguing Religion*, 105-106.

20. Wendell Berry, "Why I am Not Going to Buy a Computer," in *What are People For?* (New York: North Point Press, 2000), 171-177.

21. Marshall McLuhan, *Understanding Media: The Extensions of Man* (Cambridge, MA: The MIT Press, 1994).

22. Pew Research Center, "Most Americans Say There Is Too Much Economic Inequality in the U.S., but Fewer Than Half Call It a Top Priority," January 2020: 21.

23. For up to date data, see: *www.federalreserve.gov/releases/z1/data-viz/dfa/distribute/table/#quarter:128;series:Net%20worth;demo graphic:networth;population:all;units:shares*

24. Oxfam, "An Economy for the 99%," January 2017, Oxford: Oxfam GB for Oxfam International.

25. President's Council, *Beyond Therapy*, 279-280.

26. John Harris, "Chemical Cognitive Enhancement: Is It Unfair, Unjust, Discriminatory, or Cheating for Healthy Adults to Use Smart

Drugs?" in *The Oxford Handbook of Neuroethics*, eds. Judy Illes and Barbara J. Sahakian (Oxford: Oxford University Press, 2011), 268.

27. Bad pun. I know. Couldn't help myself.

28. John Paul II and the Ecumenical Patriarch His Holiness Bartholomew I, "Common Declaration on Environmental Ethics," June 10, 2002, *www.vatican.va*

29. Benedict XVI, *Caritas in Verite*, Encyclical Letter (2009), paragraph 69.

Chapter 4
## Fallen Dignity

1. For an account of Josef's life, see Gavan Daws, *Holy Man: Father Damien of Molokai* (O'ahu, HI: University of Hawaii Press, 1984).

2. Mother Teresa, "Acceptance Speech: The Nobel Peace Prize 1979," *www.nobelprize.org/prizes/peace/1979/teresa/acceptance-speech*.

3. For more on the life of Anjezë, see Kathryn Spink, *Mother Teresa: An Authorized Biography*, Revised and Updated Edition (New York: Harper Collins, 2011).

4. Rodney Stark, *The Rise of Christianity: A Sociologist Reconsiders History* (Princeton, NJ: Princeton University Press, 1996).

5. Tertullian, *Apology*, trans. S. Thelwall, from *Ante-Nicene Fathers*, Vol. 3., ed. Alexander Roberts, et al. (Buffalo, NY: Christian Literature Publishing Co., 1885), revised and edited for New Advent by Kevin Knight, *https://www.newadvent.org/fathers/0301.htm*: chapter 39.

6. Charles Camosy, *Losing Our Dignity: How Secularized Medicine is Undermining Fundamental Human Equality* (Hyde Park, NY: New City Press, 2021), 11-12.

7. Camosy, *Losing our Dignity*, 15.

8. Peter Singer, *Practical Ethics* (Cambridge, UK: Cambridge University Press, 1993), 111.

9. See, for example, Peter Singer, "Discussing Infanticide," *Journal of Medical Ethics* 39, 5 (2013): 260.

10. National Institute for Health and Care Excellence, *Guide to the Methods of Technology Appraisal 2013*, April 4, 2013, *www.nice.org.uk/process/pmg9*.

11. For a discussion of these data points and many others, see Edmon Awad, *et al.* "The Moral Machine Experiment," *Nature* 563 (2018): 59–64.

12. Mayo Clinic Staff, "Job Burnout: How to Spot It and Take Action," (2021), *www.mayoclinic.org/healthy-lifestyle/adult-health/in-depth/burnout/art-20046642*.

13. Camosy, *Losing our Dignity*, 63–64.

14. Quoted in Antonio Spadero, S.J., "A Big Heart Open to God: The Exclusive Interview with Pope Francis," trans. Massimo Faggioli, et al., *America*, September 30, 2013 issue: 16.

15. Catholic Church, *Catechism of the Catholic Church*, 2nd ed. (Huntingdon, PA: Our Sunday Visitor, 2000): paragraph 1850.

16. John Calvin, *Institutes of the Christian Religion*, trans. Henry Beveridge (1845): Book II, Chapter 2, paragraph 26.

17. Reinhold Niebuhr, *Man's Nature and His Communities: Essays on the Dynamics and Enigmas of Man's Personal and Social Existence* (New York: Charles Scribner's Sons, 1965), 24.

18. Joseph M. Reagle, Jr., *Hacking Life: Systemized Living and its Discontents* (Cambridge, MA: MIT Press, 2019), 2.

19. Reagle, *Hacking Life*, 4 and 3.

20. Reagle, *Hacking Life*, 13.

21. Reagle, *Hacking Life*, 13–14.

22. Reagle, *Hacking Life*, 48.

23. Reagle, *Hacking Life*, chapter 7.

24. Reagle, *Hacking Life*, 28.

25. Reagle, *Hacking Life*, 6.

26. See Dale Carnegie, *How to Win Friends and Influence People* (New York: Gallery Books, 2022).

27. Immanuel Kant, *The Moral Law: Groundwork of the Metaphysic of Morals*, trans. H.J. Paton, (London: Routledge, 2005), 8.

28. Kant, *The Moral Law*, 83.

29. Arthur Schopenhauer, *The World as Will and Representation*, volume 2, trans. E.F.J. Payne (New York: Dover, 1969), 576.

30. Some Christian outlooks flirt with the Schopenhauer Sulk. The Calvinist teaching of total depravity—not the idea that we are as bad as can be, but rather that every part of humans is depraved—has a whiff of Schopenhauer about it. But I won't wade into those debates . . . outside this passing mention in a footnote.

Chapter 5
## Enhancing Humanity

1. Plato, *Phaedrus*, in *Complete Works*, ed. John M. Cooper (Indianapolis/Cambridge: Hackett, 1997), 274b-277a.

2. President's Council, *Beyond Therapy*, 20.

3. See *www.christiantranshumanism.org/affirmation/*

4. Micah Redding, "Christian Transhumanism: Exploring the Future of Faith," in *The Transhumanism Handbook*, ed. Newton Lee (Cham, Switzerland: Springer, 2019), 779.

5. Micah Redding, "Christian Transhumanism: Exploring the Future of Faith," 782 and 783.

6. Ron Cole-Turner, "Introduction: Why the Church Should Pay Attention to Transhumanism," in *Christian Perspectives on Transhumanism and the Church*, eds. Steve Donaldson and Ron Cole-Turner (Cham, Switzerland: Palgrave Macmillan, 2018), 5. See also Ronald Cole-Turner, *The New Genesis: Theology and the Genetic Revolution* (Louisville, KY: Westminster/John Knox Press, 1993).

7. John Marshall Strahan, "Thinking Like a Christian about Transhumanism," in *The Transhumanism Handbook*, ed. Newton Lee, (Cham, Switzerland: Springer, 2019), 816.

8. Nick Bostrum, "The Fable of the Dragon-Tyrant," *The Journal of Medical Ethics* 31,5 (2005): 273-277.


Conclusion
## Enhancement and the Good Life

1. Saint Ignatius of Loyola, *Personal Writings*, trans. Joseph A. Munitiz and Philip Endean (New York: Penguin Books, 2004), 289.

2. As a starting place, I'd recommend Meghan Sullivan and Paul Blaschko, *The Good Life Method* (New York: Penguin Books, 2022).

# FOCOLARE MEDIA

*Enkindling the Spirit of Unity*

The New City Press book you are holding in your hands is one of the many resources produced by Focolare Media, which is a ministry of the Focolare Movement in North America. The Focolare is a worldwide community of people who feel called to bring about the realization of Jesus' prayer: "That all may be one" (see John 17:21).

Focolare Media wants to be your primary resource for connecting with people, ideas, and practices that build unity. Our mission is to provide content that empowers people to grow spiritually, improve relationships, engage in dialogue, and foster collaboration within the Church and throughout sociecy.

 Visit www.focolaremedia.com to learn more about all of New City Press's books, our award-winning magazine *Living City*, videos, podcasts, events and free resources.

**NEW CITY PRESS**